KW-221-232

GREEK PHRASE BOOK

This phrase book, in a handy pocket size, will help you to be readily understood on all everyday occasions; to get you quickly and easily, *where* you want and *what* you want; and to enable you to cope with those minor problems and emergencies that always seem to arise on holiday. A pronunciation guide accompanies each phrase, the topic of which can quickly be found by reference to the contents list. Subjects include: customs, medical treatment, shopping, sightseeing, restaurants, cafés and bars.

You will also find a map of the centre of Athens with the main streets given both in English and in Greek, a typical Greek menu and helpful information in each section.

TEACH YOURSELF BOOKS

GREEK
PHRASE BOOK

**I. Moschouti Green, L. Coleman
and R. Nash Newton**

TEACH YOURSELF BOOKS
Hodder and Stoughton

First printed 1980

Copyright © 1980
I. Moschouti Green, L. Coleman and R. Nash Newton

All rights reserved. No part of this publication may be reproduced
or transmitted in any form or by any means, electronic or mechan-
ical, including photocopy, recording, or any information storage
and retrieval system, without permission in writing from the pub-
lisher.

Published in the USA by David Mckay & Co. Inc.,
750 Third Avenue, New York, NY 10017, USA.

ISBN 0 340 23690 6

Phototypeset in V.I.P. Times by
Western Printing Services Ltd, Bristol.
Printed and bound in Great Britain
for Hodder and Stoughton Paperbacks,
a division of Hodder and Stoughton Ltd,
Mill Road, Dunton Green, Sevenoaks, Kent,
(Editorial Office; 47 Bedford Square, London, WC1B 3DP)
by Richard Clay (The Chaucer Press) Ltd,
Bungay, Suffolk.

Contents

Background Information

Before you set out

Any information you may require about Greece and your stay there can be sought from:

United Kingdom and Ireland
The Greek National Tourist
   Organisation (NTOG)
195-197 Regent Street,
London
W1R 8DR
Tel. 01-734-5997

United States of America
Greek National Tourist
   Organisation
645 Fifth Avenue, Olympic
   Tower
New York, NY 10.022
Tel. 42.15.777

Upon Arrival

Facilities and information concerning your stay and movement inside the country will be willingly supplied by:

1. The National Tourist Organisation of Greece (NTOG)
Head Office, 2 Amerikis (*ΑΜΕΡΙΚΗΣ*) Street, Athens. Tel. 3223-111
Information Desk, 2 Karageorgi Servias (*ΚΑΡΑΓΕΩΡΓΗ ΣΕΡ-ΒΙΑΣ*) Street, Syntagma Square, in the premises of the National Bank of Greece, Tel. 3222-545.
2. The Regional NTOG offices.
3. The Tourist Police Stations located throughout the country.

The *NTOG* in Syntagma Square, is open from 8.45 a.m. to 8 p.m. Monday through Saturday. The *Tourist Police* are available day

Using This Phrase Book

In this phrase book, we do not set out to teach you the full grammar and vocabulary necessary for holding a long conversation. Basic words and phrases will help to make you feel more at home and will create goodwill among the people of the country you are visiting, even though they may speak fluent English themselves!

These phrases, coupled with appropriate gestures and signs (such as pointing to items in a shop) should ensure that you will be understood perfectly well.

As you will see, the book is divided into various sections each dealing with everyday situations. You will also see that many of these sections repeat the same words and phrases. This means that you do not have to master a great number of new expressions in order to communicate adequately. And if you need a quick translation of a single word, there is a Reference Section and an alphabetical list of words at the back of the book.

Next to each phrase or word you will find the phonetic equivalent, the key to which is on pp. 11–14. Do remember, however, that accurate pronunciation alone is only half the battle; an appropriate gesture (or grimace) will help convey what you really mean!

An asterisk* on the left of a phrase means that this is a phrase you will need to understand but not to say yourself, *e.g.* 'Have you got anything to declare?'

We have tried to make the phrase book as comprehensive and yet as simple as possible. If you follow it carefully, it should help to make your stay in Greece enjoyable and carefree!

and night to provide tourists with information and help in all matters.

Useful information

Electric current   The power supply throughout Greece is 220 AC but in some islands and in some remote places 110 DC voltage is supplied.

Lavatories

Ladies   *ΓΥΝΑΙΚΩΝ*
Gentlemen   *ΑΝΔΡΩΝ*

Usually situated in the town or village square. In Athens, these are few and far between but you may always use the facilities provided by restaurants and cafes.

News service for foreigners
Radio: daily weather forecast and news bulletin in English 7.30–7.45 a.m.
Television: (YENED) daily news bulletin in English at 6.15 p.m.

Time   Clocks must be put forward two hours.

Worship   The predominant Church is the Greek Orthodox, but in Athens and elsewhere you may find Catholic and Protestant churches as well as Synagogues and Mosques.

Public holidays

The feasts of the Orthodox Church coincide with those of the western churches except for Easter and Whitsun which may coincide with the western dates or may fall anything up to a month later.

The principal national and religious holidays are:

January 1st	New Year's Day
January 6th	Epiphany
March 25th	National day (Commemorating the Greek Revolution in 1821)
May 1st	May Day
August 15th	Assumption of the Virgin Mary
October 28th	OHI NO Day (the historic NO to the Italian ultimatum in 1940)
December 25th	Christmas
December 26th	Boxing Day

Shrove Monday, usually early March
Good Friday to Easter Monday
Whitsun Monday, fifty days later

Closing times

Business hours vary from season to season and from district to district. Athens summer hours are as follows:

Banks	8 a.m. to 1 p.m.
Travel agencies	9 a.m. to 7 p.m.
Restaurants	noon to 3.30 p.m. and 7.30 p.m. to midnight
Cafés	8 a.m. to well after midnight
Nightclubs	9 p.m. to 5 a.m.
Cinemas	3 p.m. to midnight (open-air 8 p.m. to midnight)

Useful telephone numbers

Emergency hospital treatment	166
All night pharmacies	107
Police emergency squad	100
Fire Brigade	199
Coastguard emergency patrol	108
Road breakdown service	104
Tourist Police	171
Time	141

Index of main streets in Athens

For street names, we have used the spelling commonly found in tourists' maps which differs from the phonetic spelling in the rest of this book.

Street	Othos *ΟΔΟΣ*
Aharnón	*ΑΧΑΡΝΩΝ*
Adrianoú	*ΑΝΔΡΙΑΝΟΥ*
Ag. Konstantínou	*ΑΓ. ΚΩΝΣΤΑΝΤΙΝΟΥ*
Akadimías or	*ΑΚΑΔΗΜΙΑΣ*
(Roúzvelt)	*(ΡΟΥΖΒΕΔΤ)*
Amerikís	*ΑΜΕΡΙΚΗΣ*
Anapáfseos	*ΑΝΑΠΑΥΣΕΩΣ*
Apólonos	*ΑΠΟΛΛΩΝΟΣ*
Asklipioú	*ΑΣΚΛΗΠΙΟΥ*
Athinás	*ΑΘΗΝΑΣ*
Dion. Aeropaghítou	*ΔΙΟΝ. ΑΕΡΟΠΑΓΙΤΟΥ*
Em. Benáki	*ΕΜΜ. ΜΠΕΝΑΚΗ*
Eólou	*ΑΙΟΛΟΥ*
Ermoú	*ΕΡΜΟΥ*
Evripídou	*ΕΥΡΙΠΙΔΟΥ*

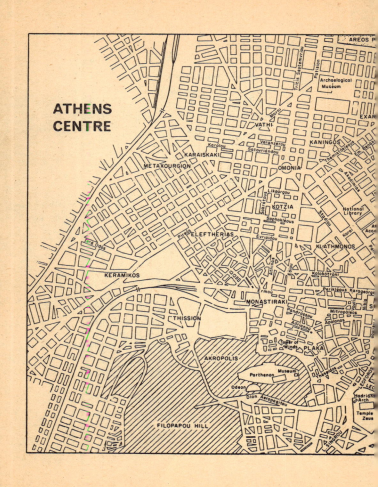

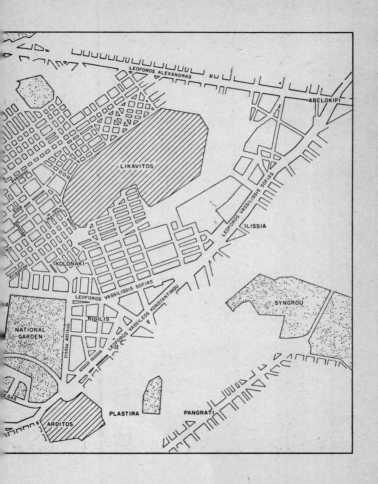

Street	**Othos** *ΟΔΟΣ*
Filelínon	*ΦΙΛΕΛΛΗΝΩΝ*
Halkokondíli	*ΧΑΛΚΟΚΟΝΔΥΛΗ*
Ierá Odós	*ΙΕΡΑ ΟΔΟΣ*
Ipokrátous	*ΙΠΠΟΚΡΑΤΟΥΣ*
Iródou Attikoú	*ΗΡΩΔΟΥ ΑΤΤΙΚΟΥ*
Karageórgi Servías	*ΚΑΡΑΓΕΩΡΓΗ ΣΕΡΒΙΑΣ*
Karólou	*ΚΑΡΟΛΟΥ*
Kolokotróni	*ΚΟΛΟΚΟΤΡΩΝΗ*
Koraí	*ΚΟΡΑΗ*
Kriezótou	*ΚΡΙΕΖΩΤΟΥ*
Likavitoú	*ΛΥΚΑΒΗΤΟΥ*
Likoúrgou	*ΛΥΚΟΥΡΓΟΥ*
Liosíon	*ΛΙΟΣΙΩΝ*
Márni	*ΜΑΡΝΗ*
Mitropóleos	*ΜΗΤΡΟΠΟΛΕΩΣ*
Níkis	*ΝΙΚΗΣ*
Omírou	*ΟΜΗΡΟΥ*
Óthonos	*ΟΘΩΝΟΣ*
Pandrósou	*ΠΑΝΔΡΟΣΟΥ*
Panepistimíou or	*ΠΑΝΕΠΙΣΤΗΜΙΟΥ*
(El Venizélou)	*(ΕΛ. ΒΕΝΙΖΕΛΟΥ)*
Patisíon or	*ΠΑΤΗΣΙΩΝ*
(28 Octovríou)	*(28ης ΟΚΤΩΒΡΙΟΥ)*
Perikléous	*ΠΕΡΙΚΛΕΟΥΣ*
Pireós	*ΠΕΙΡΑΙΩΣ*
Satovriándou	*ΣΑΤΩΒΡΙΑΝΔΟΥ*
Sína	*ΣΙΝΑ*
Sokrátous	*ΣΩΚΡΑΤΟΥΣ*
Sólonos	*ΣΟΛΩΝΟΣ*
Sophokléous	*ΣΟΦΟΚΛΕΟΥΣ*
Stadíou	*ΣΤΑΔΙΟΥ*

Street	**Othos** *ΟΔΟΣ*

Trítis Septemvríou	*3ης ΣΕΠΤΕΜΒΡΙΟΥ*
Themistokléous	*ΘΕΜΙΣΤΟΚΛΕΟΥΣ*
Théspidos	*ΘΕΣΠΙΔΟΣ*
Veranzérou	*ΒΕΡΑΝΖΕΡΟΥ*
Voulís	*ΒΟΥΛΗΣ*

Index of main avenues

Avenue	**leofóros** *ΛΕΩΦΟΡΟΣ* (abr. *ΛΕΩΦ.*)

Leofóros Alexándras	*ΛΕΩΦ. ΑΛΕΞΑΝΔΡΑΣ*
Leofóros Amalías	*ΛΕΩΦ. ΑΜΑΛΙΑΣ*
Leofóros Ólgas	*ΛΕΩΦ. ΟΛΓΑΣ*
Leofóros Vassiléos Konstantinou	*ΛΕΩΦ. ΚΩΝΣΤΑΝΤΙΝΟΥ*
Leofóros Vassilissis Sofias	*ΛΕΩΦ. ΒΑΣ. ΣΟΦΙΑΣ*
Leofóros Singroú	*ΛΕΩΦ. ΣΥΓΓΡΟΥ*

Main squares

Square	**i platía** *ΠΛΑΤΕΙΑ* (abr. *ΠΛ.*)

Omónia	*ΟΜΟΝΟΙΑ*
Sýntagma	*ΣΥΝΤΑΓΜΑ*
Monastiráki	*ΜΟΝΑΣΤΗΡΑΚΙ*
Káningos	*ΚΑΝΙΓΓΟΣ*
Klathmónos	*ΚΛΑΥΘΜΩΝΟΣ*
Kolonáki	*ΚΟΛΩΝΑΚΙ*
Kotziá	*ΚΟΤΖΙΑ*
Rigílis	*ΡΗΓΙΛΛΗΣ*

Some hills in Athens

Hill	**lófos** *ΛΟΦΟΣ*

Likavitos	*ΛΥΚΑΒΗΤΤΟΣ*
Filopápou	*ΦΙΛΟΠΑΠΠΟΥ*
Akrópolis	*ΑΚΡΟΠΟΛΙΣ*
Arditós	*ΑΡΔΗΤΟΣ*

Parks

Ethnikós Kípos
  (National Garden)   *ΕΘΝΙΚΟΣ ΚΗΠΟΣ*
Pedion tou Áreos   *ΠΕΔΙΟΝ ΤΟΥ ΑΡΕΩΣ*

Pláka (the old city)   *ΠΛΑΚΑ*

Alphabet and Pronunciation

Modern Greek uses the same alphabet as ancient Greek, but don't let this frighten you as it is relatively easy to make most of the sounds. The reading is logical and consistent, not arbitrary as it is in English. *E.G.* a's are always pronounced in the same way: as a in man and not as in table, ball, etc., as in English. There are no short and long sounds.

Remember two basic rules:

1. *All greek letters are sounded* (with very few exceptions).
2. *All words are accented* (except for a few monosyllabic ones).

It is very important that you stress firmly the accented syllable, otherwise the meaning of the word might change: *e.g.* ποτέ (**poté**) means never, while πότε; (**póte**) means when?

Marks

Accent marks: There are three accents: ώ, ὼ, ῶ. There is no difference among them as far as pronunciation is concerned. All you have to know is that you stress the accented syllable.

Breathings: (ὠ, ὡ) are little commas that go over vowels at the beginning of a word. They should be ignored as they make no difference to the pronunciation or the stress.

Punctuation marks: (;) is used for (?) and (·) is used for (;). All other punctuation marks are the same as in English.

There are twenty four letters in the Greek alphabet.

Letter			Symbol	Description
A	*a*	álpha	**(a)**	As in man.

Letter			Symbol	Description
B	β	víta	**(v)**	As in van.
Γ	γ	gh, áma	**(gh)**	As in give.
		(Before i or e)	**(y)**	As in yet.
Δ	δ	*th*élta	**(*th*)**	As in then.
E	ε	épsilon	**(e)**	As in egg.
Z	ζ	zíta	**(z)**	As in zest.
H	η	íta	**(i)**	As in meet.
Θ	θ	thíta	**(th)**	As in thin.
I	ι	yóta	**(i)**	As in meet.
K	κ	kápa	**(k)**	As in kite.
Λ	λ	lám*th*a	**(l)**	As in love.
M	μ	mí	**(m)**	As in mad.
N	ν	ni	**(n)**	As in no.
Ξ	ξ	ksi	**(ks)**	As in fox.
O	o	ómikron	**(o)**	As in hot.
Π	π	pi	**(p)**	As in post.
P	ρ	ro	**(r)**	As in red.
Σ	σ, ς	sigma	**(s)**	As in sun
T	τ	taf	**(t)**	As in top.
Y	υ	ípsilon	**(i)**	As in meet.
Φ	φ	fi	**(f)**	As in fun.
X	χ	hi	**(h)**	As in hat.
Ψ	ψ	psi	**(ps)**	As in eclipse.
Ω	ω	omégha	**(o)**	As in hot.

Vowels

All vowels are pronounced distinctly, even when they are un-stressed or at the end of the word:

$$a, ε, η, ι, o, υ, ω$$

Letter	Symbol	Description	Example		
a	(a)	As in man.	ἄλλος	**álos**	(other)
ε	(e)	As in egg.	μέρα	**méra**	(day)

Letter	Symbol	Description	Example		
η, ι, υ	(i)	As in meet.	σπίτι	**spíti**	(house)
ο, ω	(o)	As in hot.	φῶς	**fos**	(light)

Consonants

All consonants are sounded. A double consonant is pronounced as if it were single *e.g.*

ἄσσος   **(ásos)** ace.

Letter	Symbol	Description	Example		
β	(v)	As in van.	βιβλίο	**(vivlío)**	book
γ	(gh)	As in give.	γάλα	**(ghála)**	milk
(before i or e)	(y)	As in yet.	γέρος	**(yéros)**	old man
δ	(*th*)	As in then.	δάσος	**(*thásos*)**	forest
ζ	(z)	As in zest.	ζέστη	**(zésti)**	heat
θ	(th)	As in thin.	θεός	**(theós)**	God
κ	(k)	As in kite.	καλός	**(kalós)**	good
λ	(l)	As in love.	λόφος	**(lófos)**	hill
μ	(m)	As in mud.	μωρό	**(moró)**	baby
ν	(n)	As in no.	νερό	**(neró)**	water
ξ	(ks)	As in fox.	ξύλο	**(ksílo)**	wood
π	(p)	As in post.	πίνω	**(píno)**	drink
ρ	(r)	As in red.	ρίζα	**(ríza)**	root
σ, ς	(s)	As in sun.	στόμα	**(stóma)**	mouth
(before β, γ, δ, μ, ν, ρ)	(z)	As in zoo.	σμῆνος	**(zmínos)**	swarm
τ	(t)	As in top.	τόπι	**(tópi)**	ball
φ	(f)	As in fun.	φίλος	**(fílos)**	friend
χ	(h)	As in hat.	χαρά	**(hará)**	joy
ψ	(ps)	As in eclipse	ψωμί	**(psomí)**	bread

Diphthongs

Letter	Symbol	Description	Example		
αι	(e)	As in smell.	*ναί*	**(ne)**	yes
ει	(i)	As in meet.	*θεία*	**(thía)**	aunt
οι	(i)	As in meet.	*νοίκι*	**(níki)**	rent
ου	(oo)	As in cool.	*πουλί*	**(poolí)**	bird
αυ	(af)	As in after.	*αὐτό*	**(aftó)**	this
αυ	(av)	As in avenue.	*αὐλή*	**(avlí)**	yard
ευ	(ef)	As in left.	*εὐχή*	**(efhí)**	wish
ευ	(ev)	As in ever.	*νεῦμα*	**(névma)**	sign

Diaeresis: two dots placed over the second letter of a diphthong
means that the two letters are pronounced separately. *E.g.*

> *παιδί*   **pethí** (child) *but*
> *πάίδι*   **paíthi** (cutlet)

Pairs of consonants

Letter	Symbol	Description	Example		
γγ	(ng)	As in anger.	*Ἀγγλία*	**(Anglía)**	England
γκ	(g)	As in get.	*γκρεμός*	**(gremós)**	precipice
μπ	(b)	As in beer.	*μπορῶ*	**(boró)**	I can
μπ	(mb)	As in ember.	*λάμπα*	**(lámba)**	lamp
ντ	(d)	As in dog.	*ντομάτα*	**(domáta)**	tomato
ντ	(nd)	As in end.	*κέντρο*	**(kéndro)**	centre
τζ	(j)	As in John.	*τζάκι*	**(tzáki)**	fireplace
τσ	(ts)	As in lots.	*τσάντα*	**(tsánda)**	handbag

Helpful reminder on pronunciation

The letter *Δ, δ* is shown as **(th)** (in bold italics) and must be
pronounced as 'th' in the, then.

The letter Θ, θ is shown as (th) and must be pronounced as 'th' in theatre, thin.

The letter Γ, γ has two sounds:
1. Γ, γ shown as **(gh)** must be pronounced as a very soft guttural g at the back of the throat as in give.
2. Γ, γ shown as **(y)** must be pronounced as y in yet.

Remember to stress firmly the accented syllable of each word. *E.g.*

poté, póte, etc.

Stress is indicated by an accent over the stressed syllable (´).

Grammar

In modern Greek the article, noun, and adjective are all inflected and agree in gender, case and number.

There are:

> three genders (masculine, feminine, neuter)
> three cases (nominative, genitive, accusative)
> two numbers (singular, plural)

Here is an example using the three genders of the article, adjective and noun.

Masc.	*ὁ καλός Θεός*	**(o kalós theós)**	the good God
Fem.	*ἡ καλή μητέρα*	**(i kalí mitéra)**	the good mother
Neut.	*τό καλό παιδί*	**(to kaló pethí)**	the good child

We can also tell the gender of the noun by the article which precedes it.

The *articles* are:

		(a) *Definite*	(b) *Indefinite*
Masc.	*ὁ* **(o)** the	*ἕνας* **(énas)** a
Fem.	*ἡ* **(i)** the	*μία* **(mía)** a
Neut.	*τό* **(to)** the	*ἕνα* **(éna)** a

Example

Masc.	*ὁ πατέρας*	**(o patéras)**	the father
	ἕνας πατέρας	**(énas patéras)**	a father
Fem.	*ἡ μητέρα*	**(i mitéra)**	the mother
	μία μητέρα	**(mía mitéra)**	a mother
Neut.	*τό παιδί*	**(to pethí)**	the child
	ἕνα παιδί	**(éna pethí)**	a child

The definite article is also used in front of proper nouns.

Example

ὁ Πέτρος	(o Pétros)	Peter
ἡ 'Αγγλία	(i Anglia)	England
τό Λονδίνο	(to Lonthíno)	London

The definite article *the* is declined as follows:

Singular

		Masc.		Fem.		Neut.	
Nom.	the	ὁ	(o)	ἡ	(i)	τό	(to)
Gen.	of the	τοῦ	(too)	τῆς	(tis)	τοῦ	(too)
Acc.	the	τόν	(ton)	τήν	(tin)	τό	(to)

Plural

Nom.	the	οἱ	(i)	οἱ	(i)	τά	(ta)
Gen.	of the	τῶν	(ton)	τῶν	(ton)	τῶν	(ton)
Acc.	the	τούς	(toos)	τις	(tis)	τά	(ta)

The indefinite article *a* is declined as follows:

		Masc.		Fem.		Neut.	
Nom.	a (an)	ἕνας	(énas)	μία	(mía)	ἕνα	(éna)
Gen.	of a (an)	ἑνός	(enós)	μιᾶς	(myás)	ἑνός	(enós)
Acc.	a (an)	ἕνα	(éna)	μία	(mía)	ἕνα	(éna)

Note: In this book nouns are given with their articles (ὁ, ἡ, τό) to help you identify the gender.

Nouns

Masculine nouns can end in : -ος, -ας, -ης *and in plural in* -οι, -ες

Example
Singular (Nominative)

ὁ ἄνθρωπος	(o ánthropos)	the man
ὁ πατέρας	(o patéras)	the father
ὁ πολίτης	(o polítis)	the citizen

Plural (Nominative)

οἱ ἄνθρωποι	**(i ánthropi)**	the men
οἱ πατέρες	**(i patéres)**	the fathers
οἱ πολίτες	**(i polites)**	the citizens

Feminine nouns can end in: -α, -η and in plural in -ες

Example
Singular (Nominative)

ἡ πόρτα	**(i pórta)**	the door
ἡ τιμή	**(i timí)**	the price

Plural (Nominative)

οἱ πόρτες	**(i pórtes)**	the doors
οἱ τιμές	**(i timés)**	the prices

Neuter nouns can end in: -ο, -μα, -ι and in plural in -α, -τα

Example
Singular (Nominative)

τό βιβλίο	**(to vivlío)**	the book
τό στόμα	**(to stóma)**	the mouth
τό σπίτι	**(to spíti)**	the house

Plural (Nominative)

τά βιβλία	**(ta vivlía)**	the books
τά στόματα	**(ta stómata)**	the mouths
τά σπίτια	**(ta spítya)**	the houses

Adjectives

Adjectives end in:

Masc. -ος   Fem. -η or -α   Neut. -ο and in plural in:
   -οι   -ες   -α

Example
Singular (Nominative)
Masc. ὁ μικρός   **(o mikrós)**   the small

Fem.	ἡ μικρή	**(i mikrí)**	the small
Neut.	τό μικρό	**(to mikró)**	the small

Plural (Nominative)

Masc.	οἱ μικροί	**(i mikrí)**	the small
Fem.	οἱ μικρές	**(i mikrés)**	the small
Neut.	τά μικρά	**(ta mikrá)**	the small

Adjectives and nouns combined
A few examples

Singular (Nom.)

Masc.	ὁ καλός πατέρας	**(o kalós patéras)**	the good father
Fem.	ἡ καλή μητέρα	**(i kalí mitéra)**	the good mother
Neut.	τό καλό παιδί	**(to kaló pethi)**	the good child

Plural (Nom.)

Masc.	οἱ καλοί πατέρες	**(i kalí patéres)**	the good fathers
Fem.	οἱ καλές μητέρες	**(i kalés mitéres)**	the good mothers
Neut.	τά καλά παιδιά	**(ta kalá pethyá)**	the good children

Singular

Masc.	ὁ ζεστός ἥλιος	**(o zestós ílios)**	the hot sun
Fem.	ἡ καθαρή θάλασσα	**(i katharí thálassa)**	the clean sea
Neut.	τό κρύο νερό	**(to krío neró)**	the cold water

Plural

Masc.	οἱ μεγάλοι ἄνδρες	**(i ómorfes kopéles)**	the great men
Fem.	οἵ ὄμορφες κοπέλλες	**(i ómorfes kopéles)**	the beautiful girls
Neut.	τά ἀκριβά ξενοδοχεῖα	**(ta akrivá ksenothohía)**	the expensive hotels

A very useful preposition: σ' (s)

σ' combined with the article (in the accusative form) is one of the most commonly used prepositions. Used as a prefix to the definite article it becomes:

Masc.	στόν	**(ston)**
Fem.	στήν	**(stin)**
Neut.	στό	**(sto)**

and translates as: to (the), in (the), at (the), on (the), into (the)

Example

Πάω στό σινεμά
Páo sto sinema
I am going to the cinema.

'Η Ελένη είναι στό σπίτι.
i Eléni íne sto spíti
Helen is in the house.

Τό βιβλίο είναι στό πάτωμο.
to vivlio ine sto pátoma
The book is on the floor.

Πηγαίνω στό Λονδίνο.
Piyéno sto Lon*th*íno
I am going to London.

τό τραίνο είναι στό σταθμό.
To tréno íne sto stathmó.
The train is at the station.

'Η Μαρία μπαίνει στό σπίτι.
I Maria béni sto spiti.
Maria is going in to the house.

Pronouns

The Demonstrative Pronouns: this and that
The Greek for *this* is:

	Singular			Plural		
Masc.	αὐτός	(aftós)	this	αὐτοί	(aftí)	these
Fem.	αὐτή	(aftí)	this	αὐτές	(aftés)	these
Neut.	αὐτό	(aftó)	this	αὐτά	(aftá)	these

The Greek for *that* is:

	Singular			Plural		
Masc.	ἐκεῖνος	(ekínos)	that	ἐκεῖνοι	(ekíni)	those
Fem.	ἐκείνη	(ekíni)	that	ἐκεῖνες	(ekínes)	those
Neut.	ἐκεῖνο	(ekino)	that	ἐκεῖνα	(ekína)	those

Example

αὐτός ὁ δρόμος   (aftós o *th*rómos)   this street
αὐτή ἡ πόλη   (aftí i póli)   this city
αὐτό τό φόρεμα   (aftó to fórema)   this dress

Possesive Pronouns

In Greek the possessive *follows* the noun (while in English it precedes it):

ὁ φίλος μου	(o filos moo)	my friend
ὁ φίλος σου	(o filos soo)	your friend
ὁ φίλος του	(o filos too)	his friend
ὁ φίλος ·της	(o filos tis)	her friend
ὁ φίλος μας	(o filos mas)	our friend
ὁ φίλος σας	(o filos sas)	your friend
ὁ φίλος τους	(o filos toos)	their friend

Personal Pronouns

Ἐγώ	(eghò)	I
Ἐσύ	(esí)	you (familiar form)
Αὐτός	(aftós)	he
Αὐτή	(aftí)	she
Αὐτό	(aftó)	it
Ἐμεῖς	(emís)	we
Ἐσεῖς	(esís)	you (polite form)
Αὐτοί	(aftí)	they

Verbs

The verb endings show the person (I, you, he *etc.*) and so the pronoun is unnecessary before the verb, and is normally omitted.

Εἶμαι (íme) to be

Present			*Past*		
εἶμαι	(íme)	I am	ἤμουνα	(ímouna)	I was
εἶσαι	(ise)	you are	ἤσουνα	(ísouna)	you were
εἶναι	(íne)	he is	ἤτανε	(ítane)	he was
εἴμαστε	(ímaste)	we are	εἴμαστε	(ímaste)	we were
εἴσαστε	(ísaste)	you are	εἴσαστε	(ísaste)	you were
εἶναι	(íne)	they are	ἤτανε	(ítane)	they were

Ἔχω (ého) to have

Present			*Past*		
ἔχω	(ého)	I have	εἶχα	(íha)	I had
ἔχεις	(éhis)	you have	εἶχες	(íhes)	you had
ἔχει	(éhi)	he has	εἶχε	(íhe)	he had

ἔχομε	(éhome)	we have	εἴχαμε	(íhame)	we had
ἔχετε	(éhete)	you have	εἴχατε	(íhate)	you had
ἔχουν	(éhoon)	they have	εἴχανε	(íhane)	they had

Θέλω (thélo) to want

Present			Past		
θέλω	(thélo)	I want	ἤθελα	(íthela)	I wanted
θέλεις	(thélis)	you want	ἤθελες	(ítheles)	you wanted
θέλει	(théli)	he wants	ἤθελε	(íthele)	he wanted
θέλομε	(thélome)	we want	θέλαμε	(thélame)	we wanted
θέλετε	(thélete)	you want	θέλατε	(thélate)	you wanted
θέλουν	(théloon)	they want	θελανε	(thélane)	they wanted

Πάω or πηγαίνω (páo or piyéno) to go

Present			Past		
πάω	(páo)	I go	πῆγα	(pígha)	I went
πᾶς	(pas)	you go	πῆγες	(píyes)	you went
πάει	(pái)	he goes	πῆγε	(píye)	he went
πᾶμε	(páme)	we go	πήγαμε	(píghame)	we went
πᾶτε	(páte)	you go	πήγατε	(píghate)	you went
πᾶνε	(páne)	they go	πήγανε	(píghane)	they went

Κάνω (káno) to do, to make

Present			Past		
κάνω	(káno)	I do, I make	ἔκανα	(ékana)	I did, made
κάνεις	(kánis)	You do, make	ἔκανες	(ékanes)	you did, made
κάνει	(káni)	He does, makes	ἔκανε	(ékane)	he did, made
κάνομε	(kánome)	we do, make	κάναμε	(káname)	we did, make
κάνετε	(kánete)	you do, make	κάνατε	(kánate)	you did, made
κάνουν	(kánoon)	they do, make	κάνανε	(kánane)	they did, made

Ξέρω (kséro) to know

Present			Past		
ξέρω	(kséro)	I know	ἤξερα	(íksera)	I knew

ξέρεις	(kséris)	you know	ἤξερες	(íksres)	you knew
ξέρει	(kséri)	he knows	ἤξερε	(iksere)	he knew
ξέρομε	(ksérome)	we know	ξέραμε	(kvérame)	we knew
ξέρετε	(kvérete)	you know	ξέρατε	(kvérate)	you knew
ξέρουν	(kséroon)	they know	ξέρανε	(kvérane)	they knew

Μπορῶ (boró) can, to be able

Present			*Past*		
μπορῶ	(boró)	I can	μπορούσα	(boroósa)	I could
μπορεῖς	(borís)	you can	μπορούσες	(boroóses)	you could
μπορεῖ	(borí)	he can	μπορούσε	(boroóse)	he could
μπορούμε	(boroóme)	we can	μπορούσαμε	(boroósame)	we could
μπορεῖτε	(boríte)	you can	μπορούσατε	(boroósate)	you could
μποροῦν	(boroóne)	they can	μπορούσανε	(boroósane)	they could

Another very common verb is πρέπει (**prépi**) must, which does not change its endings at all.

Example

πρέπει νά πάω στήν ἐκκλησία	πρέπει νά φᾶς
Prépi na páo stin eklisía	**prépi na fas**
I must go to church	you must eat

The Future Tense is formed by adding θά (tha) before the verb.

Example

θά εἶμαι	(**tha íme**)	I shall be
θά ἔχω	(**thaého**)	I shall have
θά πάω	(**tha páo**)	I will go

The Negative is made by adding δέν (*th*en) before the verb.

Example

δέν μπορῶ	(*th*en boró)	I can't
δέν θά ἔχω	(*th*en thaého)	I shall not have
δέν θά πάω	(*th*en tha páo)	I will not go
δέν ξέρω	(*th*en kséro)	I don't know

Questions are formed simply by raising the tone of one's voice at the end of the sentence.

Example

ξέρεις;	**(kséris)**	do you know?
θά πᾶς;	**(tha pas)**	will you go?
μ'ἀγαπᾶς;	**(maghapás)**	do you love me?

Addressing people: the two kinds of 'you'

There is a familiar and a polite way of saying 'you' in Greek. Unless you know people well it is better to use the polite form ἐσεῖς **(esís)** you, which takes the second person of the verb in *plural* (and we have used this in all sections except for 'Small Talk'). With friends and children you use the familiar form ἐσύ **(esí)** you, which takes the second person of the verb *in singular*.

Example

Polite	Τ θέλετε;	**(ti thélete)**	What do you want? (2nd plur.)
Familiar	Τ θέλεις;	**(ti thélis)**	What do you want? (2nd sing.)
Polite	Τ κάνετε;	**(ti kánete)**	How are you? (2nd plur.)
Familiar	Τ κάνεις;	**(ti kánis)**	How are you? (2nd sing.)

There is nothing disastrous of course if you mix them up, you'll simply sound a little more friendly (or more polite) than you had intended.

Comparatives and superlatives

An easy way to form the comparative is by putting πιό **(pyó)** for 'more' before the adjective and ἀπό **(apó)** for 'than' after it.

Example

τό ἄσπρο κρασί εἶναι πιό ἀκριβό ἀπό τό κόκκινο
(to áspro krasí íne pyo akrinó apó to kókkino)
The white wine is more expensive than the red.

Ἔχετε πιό φθηνό κρασί;
(éhete pyó fthinó krasí)
Do you have a cheaper wine?

The superlative can be formed by just adding the definite article *the* in front of the comparative.

Example

τό ἄσπρο κρασί εἶναι τό πιό ἀκριβό
(to áspro krasí íne to pyó akrivó)
The white wine is the most expensive.

θέλω τό πιό φθηνό δωμάτιο
(thélo to pyó fthinó *th*omátio)
I want the cheapest room.

Everyday Words and Phrases

Some useful words and their opposites

Here are some useful adjectives and adverbs and their opposites; the more of them you get to know by heart, the more easily you will find you can communicate.

beautiful/ugly	**oréos/áshimos** ὡραῖος/ἄσχημος
better/worse	**kalíteros/hiróteros** καλιτερος/ χειρότερος
big/small	**meghálos/mikrós** μεγάλος/ μικρός
cheap/expensive	**fthinós/akrivós** φθηνός/ἀκριβός
clever/stupid	**éksipnos/koutós** ἔξυπνος/κουτός
early/late	**norís/arghá** νωρίς/ἀργά
easy/difficult	**éfkolos/thískolos** εὔκολος/ δύσκολος
first/last	**prótos/teleftéos** πρῶτος/ τελευταῖος
full/empty	**yemátos/áthios** γεμάτος/ἄδειος
good/bad	**kalós/kakós** καλός/κακός
heavy/light	**varis/elafrós** βαρύς/ἐλαφρός
hot/cold	**zestós/kríos** ζεστός/κρύος
near/far	**kondá/makriá** κοντά/μακρυά
old/new	**palyós/kenoóryos** παλιός/ καινούργιος
old/young	**yéros/néos** γέρος/νέος
open/closed	**aniktós/klistós** ἀνοικτός/ κλειστός
right/wrong	**sostós/láthos** σωστός/λάθος

quick/slow	**ghríghoros/arghós** *γρήγορος/ ἀργός*
vacant/occupied	**eléftheros/katiliménos** *ἐλεύθερος/κατειλημμένος*

Note: The adjectives have different endings for the masculine, feminine and neuter. We have used the masculine form here, and throughout the book, unless we indicate otherwise.

A few words which can be used with the preceding adjectives and adverbs:

very	**polí** *πολύ*
too	**parapolí** *παραπολύ*
enough	**arketá** *ἀρκετά*
a little	**lígho** *λίγο*

Example

He is very good-looking	**ine polí oréos** *εἶναι πολύ ὡραῖος*
It is too expensive	**ine parapolí akrivó** *εἶναι παραπολύ ἀκριβό*

more	**perisótero** *περισσότερο*
the most	**to pyó** *τό πιό*
less	**lighótero** *λιγότερο*
the least	**o lighótero** *ὁ λιγότερο*

Example

He is the most difficult man	**ine o pyó *th*ískolos ánthropos** *εἶναι ὁ πιό δύσκολος ἄνθρωπος*

Here is a list of words necessary for most sentences, but especially useful for directions and instructions:

after	**metá** *μετά*
also	**epísis** *ἐπίσης*
and	**ke** *καί*
at	**sto** *στό*
before	**prin** *πρίν*

behind	**píso** *πίσω*
down	**káto** *κάτω*
for	**ya** *γιά*
from	**apó** *ἀπό*
in	**mésa** *μέσα*
in front of	**brostá apó** *μπροστά ἀπό*
inside	**mésa** *μέσα*
near	**kondá** *κοντά*
next to	**thípla** *δίπλα*
of	**apó** *ἀπό*
opposite	**apénandi** *ἀπέναντι*
or	**i** *ἤ*
outside	**ékso** *ἔξω*
past	**pyó péra** *πιό πέρα*
through	**mésa apó** *μέσα ἀπό*
to	**sto** *στό*
under	**káto apó** *κάτω ἀπό*
up	**epàno** *ἐπάνω*
with	**me** *μέ*
without	**horís** *χωρίς*

Example

The cinema is near the station

To cinemá íne kondá stó stathmó
Τό σινεμά εἶναι κοντά στό σταθμό

Useful phrases

Greetings

The Greeks being very hospitable have special greetings for welcoming guests and friends. When you are visiting a Greek, he is quite likely to use one of these welcoming greetings.

	sing. (M)	**kalóstone** *Καλώστονε.*
	sing. (F)	**kalóstin** *Καλώστην.*
Welcome.	plur. (M & F)	**kalosírthate** *Καλῶς ἤρθατε.*
	plur. (M & F)	**kalosorísate** *Καλῶς ὡρίσατε.*

To which you reply:

kalós sas vríkame *Καλῶς σᾶς βρήκαμε.*

which (loosely) means that you are glad to find him well.

Another frequent greeting, used mostly among people that know each other, has to do with wishing you good health. It is an everyday casual greeting and corresponds to the English hello or the American hi.

Hi.	**ya** *Γειά.*
Hello. (sing)	**yá soo** *Γειά σου.*
(plural)	**yá sas** *Γειά σας.*

You reply in the same way.

Good morning.	**kaliméra** *Καλημέρα.*
Good evening.	**kalispéra** *Καλησπσπέρα.*
Good night.	**kaliníkta** *Καληνύκτα.*
Goodbye.	**hérete** *Χαίρετε.*
Goodbye (more familiar).	**andío** *Ἀντίο.*
See you. . . .	**tha ithothoóme** *Θά ἰδωθοῦμε.* . . .
– this evening.	– **to vráthi** – *τό βράδυ.*
– tomorrow.	– **ávrio** – *αὔριο.*
– this afternoon.	– **to apóyevma** – *τό ἀπόγενμα.*
– later.	– **arghótera** – *ἀργότερα.*

Essentials

Yes	**ne** *Ναί.*
No.	**óhi** *Ὄχι.*
Please.	**parakaló** *Παρακαλῶ.*
Thank you.	**efharistó** *Εὐχαριστῶ.*
Do you speak English?	**miláte anglikaá** *Μιλᾶτε ἀγγλικά;*
Where is . . .?	**poo íne** *Ποῦ εἶπαι . . .;*
I would like	**tha ithela** *Θά ἤθελα .*
I don't understand.	**then katalavéno** *Δέν καταλαβαίνω.*
O.K.	**endáksi** *Ἐντάξει.*

If a Greek nods his head downwards he means yes (**ne**). If he nods his head upwards he means no (**óhi**). If he shakes his head from side to side he means that he does not know.

Excuse me, may I go through?	**sighnómi, boró na peráso**
	Συγγνώμη, μπορῶ νά περάσω;
Of course/Surely.	**veveós**
	Βεβαίως.
What did you say?	**ti ípate**
	Τί εἴπατε;
I'm very sorry.	**lipáme polí**
	Λυπᾶμαι πολύ.
I beg your pardon.	**pardón/sighnomi**
	Παρντόν/συγγνώμη.
OK/That is all right.	**endáksi**
	Ἐντάξει.
Don't.	**mi**
	Μή.
Never mind/Doesn't matter.	*th*en **pirázi**
	Δέν πειράζει.

Language problems

I don't understand.	*th*en **katalavéno**
	Δέν καταλαβαίνω.
Do you speak English?	**milàte Angliká**
	Μιλᾶτε ἀγγλικά;
I don't speak Greek.	*th*en **miló Eliniká**
	Δέν μιλῶ ἑλληνικά.
Does anyone here speak English?	**milá kanís e***th***ó Angliká**
	Μιλᾶ κανείς ἐδῶ ἀγγλικά;
Please speak more slowly.	**parakaló milíste pyó arghá**
	Παρακαλῶ μιλῆστε πιό ἀργά.
What does that mean?	**ti tha pi aftó**
	Τί θά πεῖ αὐτό;

Could you translate this, please?	**boríte na metafrásete aftó, parakaló**
	Μπορεῖτε νά μεταφράσετε αὐτό, παρακαλῶ;
Yes, I understand.	**ne, katalavéno**
	Ναί, καταλαβαίνω.

Questions

Where is . . .?	**poo íne**
	Ποῦ εἶναι . . .;
Where are . . .?	**poo íne**
	Ποῦ εἶναι . . .;
What time is it?	**ti óra íne**
	Τί ὥρα εἶναι;
What is this?	**ti íne aftó**
	Τί εἶναι αὐτό;
When is . . .?	**póte íne**
	Πότε εἶναι;
How much is it?	**póso káni**
	Πόσο κάνει;
How far is . . .?	**póso makriá íne**
	Πόσο μακρυά εἶναι;
How long does it take?	**pósi óra tha pári**
	Πόση ὥρα θά πάρει;
How?	**pos**
	Πῶς;
Who?	**(M) pyós (F) pyá (N) pyó**
	Ποιός; Ποιά; Ποιό;
Why?	**yatí**
	Γιατί;
Why not?	**yatí óhi**
	Γιατί ὄχι;
What do you want?	**ti thelete**
	Τί θέλετε;
What's the matter?	**(ti tréhi) ti simvéni**
	(Τί τρέχει;) τί συμβαίνει;

Meeting people and the family

Have you met . . . . **ghnorízete**
Γνωρίζετε . . . .

– my husband? **– ton ándra moo**
– τόν ἄντρα μου;

– my wife? **– tin yinéka moo**
– τήν γυναίκα μου;

– my mother? **– tin mitéra moo**
– τήν μητέρα μου;

– my father? **– ton patéra moo**
– τόν πατέρα μου;

– my brother? **– ton athelfó moo**
– τόν ἀδελφό μου;

– my sister? **– tin athelfí moo**
– τήν ἀδελφή μου;

– my son? **– ton yió moo**
– τόν γυιό μου;

– my daughter? **– tin kóri moo**
– τήν κόρη μου;

– my friend(M)? **– ton fílo moo**
– τόν φίλο μου;

– my friend(F)? **– tin fíli moo**
– τήν φίλη μου;

How do you do? **héro polí**
Χαίρω πολύ;

This is . . . . **na sas sistíso**
Νά σᾶς συστήσω . . . .

– Mr . . . . **– ton kírio**
– τόν κύριο . . . .

– Mrs . . . . **– tin kiría**
– τήν κυρία . . . .

– Miss . . . . **– tin thespinítha**
– τήν δεσποινίδα . . . .

I am pleased to meet you. **héro polí**
Χαίρω πολύ.

How are you?	**pos ísthe** *Πῶς εἶσθε;*
Very well, thank you.	**kalá, efharistó** *καλά, εὐχαριστῶ.*

Small talk

In the following phrases we have used the 'familiar' you, more suitable for younger people in this situation.

Hello.	**yiá soo** *Γειά σου.*
What is your name?	**pos seléne** *Πῶς σέ λένε;*
I'm English.	**íme Ánglos(M) Anglitha(F)** *Εἶμαι Ἄγγλος, Αγγλίφα.*
Where do you come from?	**apo poo íse** *Ἀπό ποῦ εἶσαι;*
Do you like it here?	**soo arési ethó** *Σοῦ ἀρέσει ἐδῶ;*
I like it.	**moo arési** *Μοῦ ἀρέσει.*
I don't like it.	**then moo arési** *Δέν μοῦ ἀρέσει.*
Have you got matches?	**éhis spírta** *Ἔχεις σπίρτα;*
Do you smoke?	**kapnízis** *Καπνίζεις;*
Are you hungry?	**pinás** *Πεινᾶς;*
Are you thirsty?	**thipsás** *Διψᾶς;*
Would you like . . .?	**tha ítheles** *Θά ἤθελες . . .;*
– a drink?	**– éna potó** *– ἕνα ποτό;*

– a cigarette?	**– éna tsigháro**
	– ἕνα τσιγάρο;
– a coffee?	**– éna kafé**
	– ἕνα καφέ;
– to dance?	**– na horépsoome**
	– νά χορέψουμε;
– to go out tonight?	**– na vghoóme éxo to vráthi**
	– νά βγοῦμε ἔξω τό βράδυ;
– to go to the discotheque?	**– na páme se 'discothèque'**
	– νά πᾶμε σέ ντισκοτέκ;
Yes.	**ne**
	Ναί.
No, thank you.	**ohi, efharistó**
	Ὄχι, εὐχαριστῶ.
Would you like to go for a walk?	**páme éna perípato**
	Πᾶμε ἕνα περίπατο;
I'm tired.	**íme koorasménos(M) koorasméni(F)**
	Εἶμαι κουρασμένος, κουρασμένη.
What is your telephone number?	**ti tiléfono éhis**
	Τί τηλέφωνο ἔχεις;
Where are you staying?	**poo ménis**
	Ποῦ μένεις;
Can we meet again?	**thélis na se tho páli**
	Θέλεις νά σέ δῶ πάλι;
When?	**póte**
	Πότε;
Where?	**poo**
	Ποῦ;
Hope to see you again soon.	**elpízo na se ksanathó, poli síndoma**
	Ἐλπίζω νά σέ ξαναδῶ, πολύ σύντομα.
What a pity.	**ti kríma**
	Τί κρίμα.
Tomorrow	**ávrio**
	Αὔριο . . . .
– morning.	**– to proí**
	– τό πρωί.

– evening.	**– to vráthi**
	– τό βράδυ.
What time?	**ti óra**
	Τί ὥρα;
I love you.	**saghapó**
	Σ'ἀγαπῶ.
Good-bye.	**andío**
	Ἀντίο.

The weather

Most people go to Greece during the summer when it is very hot. If you prefer cooler weather, the spring with its abundance of wild flowers and the colourful Easter celebrations is a very good time for a visit. Autumn is also very pleasant and the temperatures are comfortable for the more arduous activities, such as mountain climbing, exploring the archaeological sites, hiking etc. In September, the **'meltemi'** the sea wind (prevalent in August) has dropped and the sea is calm, warm and soft. The summer of course is hot, dry and bright, ideal for sea-sports and lazing in the sun. Mid-summer temperatures can rise above 100°F (37.8°C) but it is a dry heat and therefore less oppressive than in countries with a humid climate. If you visit during the summer, don't forget your sun-glasses, sun hat, protective sun cream and avoid wearing nylon clothes.

The following table shows the *average* monthly temperatures in Athens, Halkidiki (Salonica) and Crete (Rethymnon) in C°:

	J	F	M	A	M	J	J	A	S	O	N	D
Athens	8.6	9.4	10.8	15.7	20.8	25.7	28.3	28.1	23.7	18.3	14.3	10.6
Salonica	6.1	7.4	10.8	14.9	19.9	24.0	26.9	26.5	22.9	17.2	11.9	8.1
Crete	12.9	13.6	14.6	17.1	20.4	24.7	26.8	27.1	24.1	21.1	18.6	15.6

Note: To convert from Centigrade to Fahrenheit, multiply by 9, divide by 5 and add 32. To convert from F° to C° subtract 32, multiply remainder by 5 and divide by 9.

Note: A daily weather forecast can be heard in English on the radio (National Programme at 6.30 p.m.).

What's the weather going to be like	**ti keró tha káni** *Τί καιρό θά κάνει . . . .*
– today?	**– símera** *– σήμερα;*
– tomorrow?	**– ávrio** *– αὔριο;*
Is it going to rain?	**tha vréksi** *Θά βρέξει;*
Is it going to be fine?	**tha káni kaló keró** *Θά κάνει καλό καιρό;*
Is it going to snow?	**tha hyonísi** *Θά χιονίσει;*
How long is this weather going to last?	**póso tha kratísi aftós o kerós** *Πόσο θά κρατήσει αὐτός ὁ καιρός;*
Is it going to get hotter?	**tha zestáni o kerós** *Θά ζεστάνει ὁ καιρός;*
Is it going to get colder?	**tha pyási krío** *Θά πιάσει κρύο;*
Is the weather going to change?	**thaláksi o kerós** *Θά ἀλλάξει ὁ καιρός;*
It's cold/hot today.	**káni krío/zésti símera** *Κάνει κρύο/ζέστη σήμερα.*
It is going to be windy.	**tha pyási aéras** *Θά πιάσει ἀέρας.*
It is very windy today.	**éhi polí aéra símera** *Ἔχει πολύ ἀέρα σήμερα.*
It's a lovely day!	**ti oréa méra!** *Τί ὡραία μέρα!*
What terrible weather!	**ti foverós kerós** *Τί φοβερός καιρός!*
What lovely weather!	**ti oréos kerós** *Τί ὡραῖος καιρός!*

On Arrival

Questions you may be asked and the answers you may need.

Customs and passport control

*Have you anything to declare?
éhete na *th*ilósete típota
Έχετε νά δηλώσετε τίποτα;

No, nothing.
óhi típota
Όχι, τίποτα.

Yes.
ne
Ναί.

*How much money do you have with you?
pósa hrímata (leptá) éhete mazí sas
Πόσα χρήματα (λεπτά) έχετε μαζί σας;

*How long will you stay?
póso keró tha mínete
Πόσο καιρό θά μείνετε;

(See Reference Section for numbers and dates)

It is for my personal use.
íne prosopikís moo hríseos
Είναι προσωπικῆς μου χρήσεως.

It isn't new.
***th*en íne kenoóryo**
Δέν εἶναι καινούργιο.

*You must pay duty on this.
prépi na plirósete telonío yaftó
Πρέπει νά πληρώσετε τελωνεῖο γι αὐτό.

*Have you anything of value?
éhete íthi aksías
Έχετε εἴδη ἀξίας;

– fur coat?
– yoóna
– γούνα,

– cine-camera?   **– kinimatoghrafikí mihaní**
     – κινηματογραφική μηχανή;

– camera?   **– fotoghrafikí mihaní**
     – φωτογραφική μηχανή;

– radio?   **– ra*th*iófono**
     – ραδιόφωνο;

– typewriter?   **– ghrafomihaní**
     – γραφομηχανή;

How to get to where you're staying

Luggage and porter

Where is the luggage from flight number . . .?   **poo íne i aposkevés apó ton arithmó ptíseos**
Πού είναι οἱ ἀποσκευές ἀπό τόν ἀριθμό πτήσεως . . .;

My bags are not here.   **i valítses moo *then* íne e*th*ó**
Οἱ βαλίτσες μου δέν εἶναι ἐδῶ.

Where is a trolley?   **poo éhi éna 'trólley'**
Πού ἔχει ἕνα τρόλλεϋ;

I want a porter.   **thélo énan ahthofóro (pörter)**
Θέλω ἕναν ἀχθοφόρο. (πόρτερ)

What is your number?   **tí arithmó éhete**
Τί ἀριθμό ἔχετε;

There is one suitcase missing.   **lípi mía valítsa**
Λείπει μιά βαλίτσα.

This is not mine.   **aftó *then* íne *th*ikó moo**
Αὐτό δέν εἶναι δικό μου.

I can't find my porter.   **then vrísko ton ahthofóro moo**
Δέν βρίσκω τόν ἀχθοφόρο μου.

His number is eight.   **éhi arithmó októ**
Ἔχει ἀριθμό ὀκτώ.

I want a taxi.   **thélo 'taxí'**
Θέλω ταξί.

I want the airline bus (the airport).	**thélo to leoforío tis eterías (too aero*th*romioo)**
	Θέλω τό λεωφορεῖο τῆς ἑταιρίας (τοῦ ἀεροδρομίου).
How much do I owe you?	**ti sas hrostó**
	Τί σᾶς χρωστῶ;
*Whatever you like.	**óti thélete**
	Ὅτι θέλετε.

Changing money at the airport

Where is the bureau de change?	**poo íne to ghrafío sinalághmatos**
	Ποῦ εἶναι τό γραφεῖο συναλλάγματος;
Where is the bank?	**poo íne i trápeza**
	Ποῦ εἶναι ἡ τράπεζα;
What is the exchange rate for sterling/dollar?	**póso éhi i líra/to *th*olário**
	Πόσο ἔχει ἡ λίρα/τό δολλάριο;

Finding transport from the airport

Where can I hire a car?	**poo boró na nikyáso éna aftokínito**
	Ποῦ μπορῶ νά νοικιάσω ἕνα αὐτοκίνητο;
Where can I get a taxi?	**poo éhi 'taxí'**
	Ποῦ ἔχει ταξί;
Where is the airlinebus?	**poo íne to leoforío tis eterías (Olymbiakís, BA etc)**
	Ποῦ εἶναι τό λεωφορεῖο τῆς ἑταιρίας; (Ὀλυμπιακῆς, κ.λ. π)
Is there a bus for . . .?	**éhi leoforío ya**
	Ἔχει λεωφορεῖο γιά . . .;
What time does it go?	**ti óra févyi**
	Τί ὥρα φεύγει;
When is the next one?	**póte íne to epómeno**
	Πότε εἶναι τό ἐπόμενο;

Fares

(Bus) What is the fare to	**póso éhi to isitírio ya**
	Πόσο ἔχει τό εἰσιτήριο γιά ....
(Taxi) How much would it be to take me to ...? About	**póso thélete ya na me páte sto ... perípoo**
	Πόσο θέλετε γιά νά μέ πᾶτε στό ...; Περίπν ....
How much is it?	**póso káni**
	Πόσο κάνει;

Note: Airport buses will take you to Syntagma Square (Constitution Square) in Athens or to 96 Syngrou (*ΣΥΓΓΡΟΧ*) Street, the Olympic Airways Offices.

At the Hotel

Hotels are classified in six categories: L,A,B,C,D and E according to level of comfort and service offered. D and E classes, usually not mentioned by travel agencies, are clean but very simple. They should really come under the heading of 'roughing it'.

Checking In

Good-day.
hérete
Χαίρετε.

*What is your name?
pos léyesthe
Πῶς λέγεστε;

I am Mr/Mrs/Miss . . . .
íme o kírios/i kiría/i *t*hespinís
Εἶμαι ὁ κύριος/ἡ κυρία/ἡ δεσποινίς . . . .

I have a reservation.
ého kratísi *t*homátio
Ἔχω κρατήσει δωμάτιο.

I haven't a reservation.
***t*hen ého kratísi *t*homátio**
Δέν ἔχω κρατήσει δωμάτιο.

Have you a room for tonight?
éhete *t*homátio ya símera to vra*t*hi
Ἔχετε δωμάτιο γιά σήμερα τό βράδυ;

Can you suggest another hotel?
ksérete kanéna álo kseno*t*hohío
Ξέρετε κανένα ἄλλο ξενοδοχεῖο;

*How long do you want to stay?
póses méres tha mínete
Πόσες μέρες θά μείνετε;

I want to stay for . . . days/weeks
thélo na míno ya . . . méres/ ev*t*homáthes
Θέλω νά μείνω γιά . . . μέρες/ ἑβδομάδες

Do you have a single room?
éhete éna monóklino *t*homatio
Ἔχετε ἕνα μονόκλινο δωμάτιο;

Do you have a room . . .?

éhete éna *th*omátio
Ἔχετε ἕνα δωμάτιο . . .;

– with a double bed?

– ména *th*ipló kreváti
– μ'ἕνα διπλό κρεββάτι;

– with twin beds?

– me *th*ío monà krevátia
– μέ δύο μονά κρεββάτια;

– with a bath?

– me bányo
– μέ μπάνιο;

– without a bath?

– horís bányo
– χωρίς μπάνιο;

– with shower?

– me doós
– μέ ντούς;

– with wash-basin?

– me niptíra
– μέ νιπτήρα;

– with hot-water?

– me zestó neró
– μέ ζεστό νερό;

How much is the room per night/ week?

póso káni to *th*omátio tin iméra/ tin ev*th*omátha
Πόσο κάνει τό δωμάτιο τήν ἡμέρα/ τήν ἑβδομάδα;

– with three meals (full board)?

– me ta tría yévmata ('full pensión')
– μέ τά τρία γεύματα (φουλ πανσιόν);

– with two meals (half board)?

– me ta *th*ío yévmata ('demí- pensión')
– μέ τά δύο γεύματα (ντεμι- πανσιόν);

– for bed and breakfast?

– me to proinó móno
– μέ τό πρωινό μόνο;

Do you make any reduction for children/the baby?

kánete ékptosi ya ta pe*th*yá/ya to moró
Κάνετε ἔκπτωση γιά τά παιδιά/γιά τό μωρό;

Have you a less expensive room?

éhete álo *th*omátio pyó fthinó
Ἔχετε ἄλλο δωμάτιο πιό φθηνό;

Could we have a cot for the baby?	**boríte na mas válete éna krevatáki ya to moró** *Μπορεῖτε νά μᾶς βάλετε ἕνα κρεββατάκι γιά τό μωρό;*
Could we have an extra bed for the child?	**boríte na válete éna akomi kreváti ya to pethí** *Μπορεῖτε νά βάλετε ἕνα ἀκόμη κρεββάτι γιά τό παιδί;*
Do we pay extra for it?	**tha plirósoome éxtra yaftó** *Θά πληρώσουμε ἔξτρα γι 'αὐτό;*
I would like a room	**tha íthela éna thomátio** *Θά ἤθελα ἕνα δωμάτιο . . . .*
– on the ground floor.	**– sto isóyio** *– στό ἰσόγειο.*
– on the top floor.	**– sto teleftéo pátoma** *– στό τελευταῖο πάτωμα.*
– with a view of the sea.	**– me théa pros tin thálasa** *– μέ θέα πρός τήν θάλασσα.*
I would like a	**tha íthela éna** *Θά ἤθελα ἕνα . . . .*
– quiet room.	**– ísiho thomátio** *– ἥσυχο δωμάτιο.*
– cool room.	**– throseró thomátio** *– δροσερό δωμάτιο.*
Can I see the room first please?	**boró na to tho próta to thomátio parakaló** *Μπορῶ νά το δῶ πρῶτα τό δωμάτιο παρακαλῶ;*
I like it, I'll take it.	**moo arési tha to páro** *Μοῦ ἀρέσει, θά τό πάρω.*
I don't like it, it is very	**then moo arési íne polí** *Δέν μοῦ ἀρέσει, εἶναι πολύ . . . .*
– hot.	**– zestó** *– ζεστό.*
– dark.	**– skotinó** *– σκοτεινό.*

– small.

– mikró
– μικρό.

– expensive.

– akrivó
– ἀκριβό.

It is too noisy.

éhi polí thórivo
Ἔχει πολύ θόρυβο.

Where is . . . .

poo íne
Ποῦ εἶναι . . . .

– the lift?

– to asansér
– τό ἀσανσέρ;

– the dining-room?

– i trapezaría
– ἡ τραπεζαρία;

– the lavatory?

– i tooaléta
– ἡ τουαλέττα;

Meals
What time is . . . .

ti óra íne
Τί ὥρα εἶναι . . . .

– breakfast?

– to proinó
– τό πρωινό;

– lunch?

– to mesimerianó
– τό μεσημεριανό;

– dinner?

– to vrathinó
– τό βραδυνό;

Can I have breakfast in my room?

boró na eho to proinó sto thomatió moo
Μπορῶ νά ἔχω τό πρωινό στό δωμάτιο μου;

Room Service
Please send up . . . .

parakaló stílte epáno
Παρακαλῶ στεῖλτε ἐπάνω . . . .

– one coffee, two coffees.

– éna kafé thío kaféthes
– ἕνα καφέ, δύο καφέδες.

– tea for three.

– tsái ya tris
– τσάϊ γιά τρεῖς.

– iced water.

– paghoméno neró
– παγωμένο νερό

– bottled (mineral) water.

**– botilyarisméno
(metalikó) neró**
– μποτιλιαρισμὲνο (μεταλλικό)
νερό.

Mineral water is usually asked for, by its brand name **neró Sáriza,
Karandáni lootrakíoo, Ívi etc.**

– a bottle of red/white wine.

– éna bookáli kókino/áspro krasí
– ἕνα μπουκάλι κόκκινο/ἄσπρο
κρασί.

– ice-cream, vanilla/chocolate.

– paghotó kréma/sokoláta
– παγωτό κρέμα/σοκολάτα.

General
Can I drink the water from the
tap?

to neró tis vrísis pínete
Τό νερό τῆς βρύσης πίνεται;

Where can I park my car?

poo na parkáro to aftokínitó moo
Ποῦ νά παρκάρω τό αὐτοκίνητό
μου;

What time does the hotel close at
night?

**ti óra klíni to ksenothohío to
vráthi**
Τί ὥρα κλείνει τό ξενοδοχεῖο τό
βράδυ;

At the reception desk
Can I have my key please?

to klithí moo parakaló
Τό κλειδί μου παρακαλῶ;

*What room number do you
have?

ti arithmó thomatíoo éhete
Τί ἀριθμό δωματίου ἔχετε;

I've lost my key.

éhasa to klithí moo
Ἔχασα τό κλειδί μου.

Could you give me the key to the
bathroom please?

moo thínete to klithí too bányoo
Μοῦ δίνετε τό κλειδί τοῦ μπάνιου,
παρακαλῶ;

Are there any letters for me?
ého ghrámata
Ἔχω γράμματα;

Any messages for me?
típota paragelíes ya ména
Τίποτα παραγγελίες γιά μένα;

Please wake me up at six tomorrow morning.
parakaló na me ksipnísete stis éksi to proí
Παρακαλῶ νά μέ ξυπνήσετε στις ἕξι τὸ πρωί.

The . . . does not work.
hálase
Χάλασε . . .

– light
– to fos
– τό φῶς

– heating
– i thérmansi
– ἡ θέρμανση

– air conditioning
– to 'air condition'
– τό ἔαρ κοντίσιον

– the socket
– i príza
– ἡ πρίζα

– the lock
– i klitharyá
– ἡ κλειδαριά

The light is very poor.
to fos íne polí mikró
Τό φῶς εἶναι πολύ μικρό.

There is no hot water.
then éhi zestó neró
Δέν ἔχει ζεστό νερό.

There is no electricity.
then éhi ilektrikó
Δέν ἔχει ἠλεκτρικό.

The toilet doesn't work.
i tooaléta then litooryí
Ἡ τουαλέττα δέν λειτουργεῖ.

The wash basin is blocked.
o niptíras íne vooloménos
Ὁ νιπτήρας εἶναι βουλλωμένος.

I have a few things to be laundered.
ého meriká roóha ya plísimo
Ἔχω μερικά ροῦχα γιά πλύσιμο.

When will they be ready?
póte tha íne étima
Πότε θά εἶναι ἕτοιμα;

Tomorrow.
ávrio
Αὔριο.

Would you clean these shoes please?	**moo katharízete aftá ta papoótsya parakaló** *Μοῦ καθαρίζετε αὐτά τά παπούτσια παρακαλῶ;*
Would you press this please?	**moo si*th*erónete aftó parakaló** *Μοῦ σιδερώνετε αὐτό παρακαλῶ;*

When someone knocks at the door

Come in.	**embrós** *'Εμπρός.*
Please wait a moment.	**perimónete éna leptó** *Περιμένετε ἕνα λεπτό.*
Please come back later.	**parakaló eláte arghótera** *Παρακαλῶ ἐλᾶτε ἀργότερα.*

If you need something

Please bring me	**parakaló moo *th*ínete** *Παρακαλῶ μοῦ δίνετε . . . .*
– an ashtray.	**– éna tasáki** *– ἕνα τασάκι.*
– a blanket.	**– mía koovérta** *– μία κουβέρτα.*
– some coathangers.	**– merikés kremástres** *– μερικές κρεμάστρες.*
– a needle and thread.	**– mía velóna ke klostí** *– μία βελόνα καί κλωστή.*
– a pillow.	**– éna maksilári** *– ἕνα μαξιλάρι.*
– a sheet.	**– éna sendóni** *– ἕνα σεντόνι.*
– some soap.	**– sapoóni** *– σαπούνι.*
– toilet paper.	**– hartí tooalétas** *– χαρτί τουαλέττας.*
– a towel.	**– mía petséta** *– μία πετσέτα.*

– a jug of iced water.

– **éna kanáti paghoméno neró**
– ἕνα κανάτι παγωμένο νερό.

– some hot water for shaving.

– **lígho zestó neró ya ksírisma**
– λίγο ζεστό νερό γιά ξύρισμα.

At reception on leaving

Please may I have the bill?

parakaló moo *thí*nete ton logharyasmó
Παρακαλῶ μοῦ δίνετε τόν λογαριασμό;

I think you made a mistake in the bill.

nomízo óti éhete éna láthos ston logharyasmó
Νομίζω ὅτι ἔχετε ἕνα λάθος στόν λογαριασμό.

Is everything included?

íne óla mésa
Εἶναι ὅλα μέσα;

Service too?

to posostó ipiresías
Τό ποσοστό ὑπηρεσίας;

Can I have a receipt?

boríte na moo *thó*sete mía apó*th*iksi
Μπορεῖτε νά μοῦ δώσετε μία ἀπόδειξη;

Will you have my letters sent on, to this address, please.

boríte na moo stílete ta ghrámata moo saftí tin *th*iéf*th*insi parakaló
Μπορεῖτε νά μοῦ στείλετε τά γράμματα μου σ'αὐτή τήν διεύθυνση, παρακαλῶ.

I'm leaving today.

févgho símera
Φεύγω σήμερα.

I'm leaving tomorrow.

tha fígho ávrio
Θά φύγω αὔριο.

Could you order a taxi for ten in the morning?

moo kanonízete éna 'taxi' ya tis *th*éka to proí
Μοῦ κανονίζετε ἕνα ταξί γιά τίς δέκα τό πρωί;

Please could someone bring my bags down?	**péste na moo katevásoon tis valítses moo parakaló**
	Πέστε, νά μοῦ κατεβάσουν τίς βαλίτσες μου, παρακαλῶ;
This is for you (tip).	**aftó ya sas**
	Αὐτό γιά σᾶς.
Many thanks, goodbye.	**efharistó polí, hérete**
	Εὐχαριστῶ πολύ, χαίρετε.

USEFUL SIGNS

ΩΘΗΣΑΤΕ **othísate**	push
ΣΥΡΑΤΕ **sírate**	pull
ΘΕΡΜΟ **thermó**	hot
ΨΥΧΡΟ **psihró**	cold

Camping and Caravanning

Absence of rain and freedom to camp anywhere (except near archaeological sites or built-up areas) make camping the easiest and cheapest way to see the country. The official policy, however, is to discourage freelance camping.

The NTOG, the Hellenic Touring Club and several individuals have set up camping grounds in the most attractive parts of the country. Some of them stay open all year round. Most are excellently equipped. A list of the sites, the amenities offered in each, and the prices charged can be obtained from the *NTOG* and the Hellenic Touring Club, 12 Politechniou (*ΠΟΛΥΤΕΧΝΙΟΥ*) Street in Athens (tel. 5248-600).

May we camp here?	**boroóme na kataskinósoome e*th*ó**
	Μπορούμε νά κατασκηνώσουμε ἐδῶ;
Where is the nearest camp site?	**poó éhi kataskínosi e*th*ó kondá**
	Ποῦ ἔχει κατασκήνωση ἐδῶ κοντά;
Is there a camp-site near . . .?	**ehi 'camping' kondá sto/stin**
	Ἔχει κάμπιγκ κοντά στό/στήν . . .;
How much is it	**póso káni**
	Πόσο κάνει . . . .
– per night?	**– tin iméra**
	– τήν ἡμέρα;
– per person?	**– to átomo**
	– τό ἄτομο;
– per week?	**– tin ev*th*omát*h*a**
	– τήν ἑβδομάδα;
– for the caravan?	**– ya to trohóspito**
	– γιά τό τροχόσπιτο;

– for the car?	**– ya to aftokínito**
	– *γιά τό αὐτοκίνητο;*
Are there	**éhi**
	Ἔχει . . . .
– lavatories?	**– tooalétes**
	– *τουαλέττες;*
– showers?	**– doós**
	– *ντούς;*
– hot water?	**– zestó neró**
	– *ζεστό νερό;*
– telephone?	**– tiléfono**
	– *τηλέφωνο;*
– launderette?	**– plindírio**
	– *πλυντήριο;*
– cafeteria?	**– 'cafetéria'**
	– *καφετήρια;*
– bar?	**– 'bar'**
	– *μπάρ;*
Can we hire a tent?	**boroóme na nikyásoome mía skiní (ténda)**
	Μπορούμε νά νοικιάσουμε μιά σκηνή (τέντα);
Where can I buy . . .?	**poo boró naghoráso**
	Πού μπορῶ ν'ἀγοράσω . . .;
May we light a fire?	**boroóme nanápsoome fotyá**
	Μπορούμε ν'ἀνάψουμε φωτιά;
Where do I put the rubbish?	**poó boró na petákso ta skoopíthya**
	Πού μπορῶ νά πετάξω τά σκουπίδια;
Is this drinking water?	**íne pósimo aftó to neró**
	Εἶναι πόσιμο, αὐτό τό νερό;

USEFUL SIGNS

ΑΠΑΓΟΡΕΥΕΤΑΙ ΤΟ ΚΑΜΠΙΝΓΚ	Camping forbidden

ΑΠΑΓΟΡΕΥΟΝΤΑΙ ΤΑ ΤΡΟΧΟΣΠΙΤΑ	No caravans
ΟΙ ΠΑΡΑΒΑΤΕΣ ΘΑ ΔΙΩΧΘΟΥΝ	Trespassers will be prosecuted
ΠΟΣΙΜΟ ΝΕΡΟ	Drinking water
ΜΗ ΠΟΣΙΜΟ ΝΕΡΟ	Not drinking water
ΑΠΑΓΟΡΕΥΕΤΑΙ Η ΕΙΣΟΔΟΣ	No entry

Youth Hostelling

Youth hostels are run by:

1. *The Greek Youth Hostel Association* at 4 Dragatsaniou (*ΔΡΑΓΑΤΣΑΝΙΟΥ*) Street in Athens (Tel. 3234-107), affiliated to the International Youth Hostel Federation. Members are admitted to its hostels throughout the country. They will also supply non-members with the requisite card and accept applications for an advance reservation. Meals are provided, maximum stay is five nights, and there is no age limit as to who can stay at the youth hostel.

2. *YMCA* (ΧΑΝ in Greek), 28 Omirou and Akadimias (*ΟΜΗΡΟΥ* and *ΑΚΑΔΗΜΙΑΣ*) Street, Athens (Tel. 3626-970). Maximum stay in the hostels is ten nights and restricted to holders of international YMCA cards

3. *YWCA* (ΧΕΝ in Greek) 11 Amerikis Street (*ΑΜΕΡΙΚΗΣ*) (Tel. 3624-291). Membership not necessary; stays are limited to twenty nights.

The · *Greek Alpine Association* at 7 Karageorgi Servias (*ΚΑΡΑΓΕΩΡΓΗ ΣΕΡΒΙΑΣ*) Street, Athens (Tel. 3234-555) maintains refuge huts on mountains.

Almost everywhere simple accommodation is available in private houses at low prices. Inquiries should be made to the Tourist Police in the area concerned.

In Athens, there is a large number of low-priced pensions. Most are between Syntagma Square and Plaka, many are on Nikis (*ΝΙΚΗΣ*) Street.

Is there a Youth Hostel near here? **éhi 'Youth Hostel' ethó kondá**
Έχει Γιούθ Χόστελ ἐδῶ κοντά;

Is there a YMCA/YWCA near here?

éhi ksenóna tis HAN/HEN e*th***ó kondá**
Ἔχει Ξενώνα τῆς ΧΑΝ/ΧΕΝ ἐδῶ κοντα;

I'd like to stay for a night/a week.

tha íthela na míno ya mía méra/ mía ev*th***omá***th***a**
Θά ἤθελα νά μείνω γιά μιά μέρα/ μία ἑβδομάδα.

*You can only stay one night.

boríte na mínete móno mía níkta
Μπορεῖτε νά μείνετε μόνο μιά νύκτα.

*Do you have a student-card?

éhete fititikí taftótita
Ἔχετε φοιτητική ταυτότητα;

I'd like a . . .

tha íthela
Θά ἤθελα . . . .

– sleeping-bag.

– éna 'sleeping-bag'
– ἕνα σλίπιγκ-μπάγκ.

– blanket.

– mía koovérta
– μιά κουβέρτα.

– packed lunch.

– 'sandwich' ya na ta páro mazí moo
– σάντουϊτς γιά νά τά πάρω μαζί μου.

Where can I leave . . . .

poo boró nafíso
Ποῦ μπορῶ ν'ἀφήσω . . . .

– this?

– aftó
– αὐτό;

– my rucksack?

– to saki*th***io moo**
– τό σακκίδιο μου;

– my bicycle?

– to po*th***ílato moo**
– τό ποδήλατό μου;

What time must we be out in the morning?

ti óra prépi na fíghoome to proí
Τί ὥρα πρέπει νά φύγουμε τό πρωί;

What time must we be in at night?

ti óra prépi na yirísoome to vra*th***i**
Τί ὥρα πρέπει νά γυρίσουμε τό βράδυ;

Do you give meals?   **thínete yévmata**
Δίνετε γεύματα;

*Only breakfast.   **móno to proinó**
Μόνο τό πρωϊνό.

Where else can we stay   **poo aloó boroóme na mínoome**
(cheaply)?   **(poo na min íne akrivá)**
Ποῦ ἀλλοῦ μποροῦμε νά μείνουμε
(ποῦ νά μήν εἶναι ἀκριβά);

How far is the next village?   **póso makríá íne to epómeno horyó**
Πόσο μακρυά εἶναι τό ἐπόμενο
χωριό;

Travelling

At the mainline station

The railway network is operated by *ΟΣΕ* (OSE) (Hellenic Railways Organisation) whose head office is at 1–3 Karolou Street (*ΚΑΡΟΛΟΥ*) Athens, (Tel. 5222-491).

Ticket office is at 6 Sina (*ΣΙΝΑ*) Street Athens, (Tel. 3624-402).

Recorded timetable information Tel. 145.

There are two main line stations in Athens very close to each other:

1. *ΣΤΑΘΜΟΣ ΛΑΡΙΣΣΗΣ* (**Stathmós Laríssis**) for trains going to Northern Greece and abroad.

2. *ΣΤΑΘΜΟΣ ΠΕΛΟΠΟΝΝΗΣΟΥ* (**Stathmós Peloponísou**) for trains going South, to the Peloponnese. Trains are comfortable and on time and not expensive.

Note: Train schedules and tickets can also be obtained from travel agents. Train schedules also available at NTOG.

Note: Students with the international student card may travel on the OSE network at half price.

I'd like a ticket to	**thélo éna isitírio ya** *Θέλω ἕνα εἰσιτήριο γιά ....*
I'd like a *return* ticket to	**thélo éna isitírio metepistrofís ya** *Θέλω ἕνα εἰσιτήριο μετ'ἐπιστροφῆς* *γιά ....*
*First or second class?	**próti i théfteri thési** *Πρώτη ἤ δεύτερη θέση;*

Does the child pay the full fare?	**to pe*th*í pliróni olókliro isitírio**
	Τό παιδί πληρώνει ὁλόκληρο εἰσιτήριο;
*How old is he?	**póso hronón íne**
	Πόσο χρονῶν εἶναι;
Can I reserve a seat?	**boró na kratíso mía thési**
	Μπορῶ νά κρατήσω μιά θέση;
What is the number of my seat?	**ti arithmó éhi i thési moo**
	Τί ἀριθμό ἔχει ἡ θέση μου;
I'd like a seat	**thélo mía thési**
	Θέλω μία θέση . . . .
– facing the engine.	**– poo na vlépi prós tin mihaní**
	– ποὺ νά βλέπει πρός τήν μηχανή.
– with my back to the engine.	**– andítheta apó tin mihaní**
	– ἀντίθετα ἀπό την μηχανή.
– by the window.	**– kondá sto paráthiro**
	– κοντά στό παράθυρο.
– aisle seat.	**– kondá sto *th*yathromo**
	– κοντά στό διαδρομο.
Has the train got a	**éhi to tréno**
	Ἔχει τό τραῖνο . . . .
– dining-car?	**– vagón-restauránt**
	– βαγκόν-ρεστωράν;
– buffet?	**– 'buffét'**
	– μπουφέ;
– sleeping car?	**– vagon-li**
	– βαγκόν-λί;
May I reserve a berth in the sleeping-car?	**boró na kratíso mía couchét sto vagón-li**
	Μπορῶ νά κρατήσω μιά κουσέτ στό βαγκόν-λί;
How much does it cost?	**póso káni**
	Πόσο κάνει;
What time does the train leave for . . .?	**ti óra févyi to tréno ya**
	Τί ὥρα φεύγει τό τραῖνο γιά . . . ,
What time does the train arrive from . . .?	**ti óra fth áni to tréno apó**
	Τί ὥρα φτάνει τό τραῖνο ἀπό . . .;

When does it get to . . .?

póte tha fthási sto/sti
Πότε θά φτάει στό/στή . . .;

Does it stop at . . .?

stamatái sto/sti
Σταματάει στό/στή . . .;

Is this the right train for . . .?

pái aftó to tréno sto/sti
Πάει αὐτό τό τραῖνο στό/στή . . .;

Is it the express?

íne i tahía
Εἶναι ἡ ταχεία;

Must I change train for . . .?

prépi nalákso tréno ya
Πρέπει ν'ἀλλάξω τραῖνο γιά . . .

Where do I change for . . .?

poo prépi nalákso tréno ya
*Πού πρέπει ν'ἀλλάξω τραῖνο
γιά . . .;*

What time is the first/last train for . . .?

ti óra févyi to próto/teleftéo tréno ya
*Τί ὥρα φεύγει τό πρῶτο/τελευταῖο
τραῖνο γιά . . .;*

Have I missed the train for . . .?

éhasa to tréno ya
Ἔχασα τό τραῖνο γιά . . .;

What time is the next one?

ti óra íne to epómeno
Τί ὥρα εἶναι τό ἑπόμενο;

May I have a timetable please?

moo thínete éna thromológio parakaló
*Μοῦ δίνετε ἕνα δρομολόγιο
παρακαλῶ;*

Is this seat taken?

íne piasméni aftí i thési
Εἶναι πιασμένη αὐτή ἡ θέση;

I think this is my seat.

nomízo óti aftí íne i thési moo
Νομίζω ὅτι αὐτή εἶναι ἡ θέση μου.

Please could you mind my seat/things?

parakaló, moo filáyete tin thési moo/ta prághmatá moo
*Παρακαλῶ, μοῦ φυλάγετε τήν θέση
μου/τά πράγματά μου;*

I shall pay the excess.

tha plíroso tin thiaforá
Θά πληρώσω τήν διαφορά.

Will you tell me when we arrive at . . .?

tha moo píte ótan tha fthásome sto
*Θά μοῦ πεῖτε ὅταν θά φτάσομε
στό . . .;*

STATION SIGNS

ΕΙΣΙΤΗΡΙΑ isitíria	Tickets
ΠΛΗΡΟΦΟΡΙΑΙ pliroforíe	Information
ΤΗΛΕΦΩΝΟ tiléfono	Telephone
ΑΙΘΟΥΣΑ ΑΝΑΜΟΝΗΣ éthousa anamonís	Waiting room
ΑΠΟΣΚΕΥΑΙ aposkevé	Luggage
ΑΝΔΡΩΝ an*th*rón	Gentlemen
ΓΥΝΑΙΚΩΝ yinekón	Ladies
ΕΙΣΟΔΟΣ íso*th*os	Entrance
ΕΞΟΔΟΣ ékso*th*os	Exit
ΑΠΑΓΟΡΕΥΕΤΑΙ Η ΕΙΣΟΔΟΣ apaghorévete i íso*th*os	No Entrance
ΑΠΑΓΟΡΕΥΕΤΑΙ ΤΟ *ΚΑΠΝΙΖΕΙΝ* apaghorévete to kapnízin	No Smoking
ΑΝΑΧΩΡΗΣΕΙΣ anahorísis	Departures
ΑΦΙΞΕΙΣ afíksis	Arrivals
ΜΗΝ ΕΓΓΙΖΕΤΕ min egízete	Do not Touch
ΚΙΝΔΥΝΟΣ ΘΑΝΑΤΟΣ kín*th*inos thánatos	Deadly Danger
ΚΙΝΔΥΝΟΣ kín*th*inos	Danger

On the underground

The underground *Ο ΗΛΕΚΤΡΙΚΟΣ* (**ó ilektrikís**) or *Ο ΥΠΟΓΕΙΟΣ* (**ó ipóyios**).

An easy way for getting to Piraeus to catch a boat to the islands, or for going to Kifissia, a cool leafy suburb of Athens.

It starts at 5.30 a.m. and goes on till 12.30 a.m. It is quite easy to use as there is only one line and the trains run frequently. The whole journey takes just over an hour.

Here are some of the stations you might use, marked with a star (*).

*ΠΕΙΡΑΙΕΥΣ	PIRAEUS (the port of Athens), also know as Pireás
Ν. ΦΑΛΗΡΟΝ	N. PHALIRON
ΜΟΣΧΑΤΟΝ	MOSHATON
ΚΑΛΛΙΘΕΑ	KALITHEA
ΠΕΤΡΑΛΩΝΑ	PETRALONA
*ΘΗΣΕΙΟΝ	THISSION (for visiting archaeological sites)
*ΜΟΝΑΣΤΗΡΙΟΝ	MONASTIRION (flea market and interesting shopping) also known as MONASTIRAKI
*ΟΜΟΝΟΙΑ	OMONIA (Athens Central Square)
*ΒΙΚΤΩΡΙΑ	VICTORIA (pleasant square with a park near by)
*ΑΤΤΙΚΗ	ATTIKI (the nearest stop to the two Railway Stations)

Nine more stops before you get to:

*ΚΗΦΙΣΣΙΑ	KIFISSIA (the last stop and a pleasant suburb)

Does this train go to Piraeus? **pái aftó to tréno ston Pireá**
Πάει αὐτό τό τραῖνο στόν Πειραιά;

I want a ticket to Monastiraki.   **thélo éna isitírio ya to
       Monastiráki**
       *Θέλω ἕνα εἰσιτήριο γιά τό
       Μοναστηράκι.*

How much is it?   **póso káni**
       Πόσο κάνει;

Note: There is a map showing the stations, inside the train compartments.

On the bus

Buses (Provinces and Islands)
The railway network is efficiently complemented by buses which reach even the remotest village. Even the Ionian Islands are served by an integrated bus-ferry system. Buses are frequent and fast, not expensive and full of local interest.

KTEL Buses (for Provinces and Islands) have two main bus terminals in Athens:
       1.   at 100 Kifissoú Street (*ΚΗΦΙΣΣΟΥ*).
       2.   at 260 Liossíon Street (*ΛΙΟΣΙΩΝ*).

OSE Buses
OSE also operates buses throughout Greece. Buses for Northern Greece leave from Larissis Railway Station (Tel. 8213-882). Buses for Southern Greece leave from the Peloponnese Railway Station (Tel. 5131-636).

Note: Information on routes throughout Greece is also supplied by the NTOG.

By coach
Many travel agencies run tours all over Greece, in luxurious coaches called 'pullman'. These are used mostly by the tourists.

     These tours range from half-day sight-seeing in Athens to many days' fully organised excursions to the whole of Greece.

By Bus or Trolley-bus (urban routes)

Public transport in Athens is very frequent, cheap and around rush hours very crowded. You enter (or push your way in) from the back door, where you pay, and you get out from the front door. There is usually a fixed fare to the centre of Athens (Omonia Square); if you want to stay on, after Omonia, ask for a 'sinéhia' (*συνέχεια*) which is a continuation ticket.

Children pay full fare if they are over four, otherwise they travel free. Smoking is not allowed in the buses or the underground.

Seaside places such as Pháliron, Glyfáda, Voúla, Vouliagméni and Várkiza are all on the urban bus routes and can be easily reached.

Buses usually run till midnight; a full schedule for the Athens bus services can be easily obtained from the NTOG.

Bus stop	**stásis**
	ΣΤΑΣΙΣ
Where do I get the bus (the trolley) for . . .?	**poo tha páro to leoforío (trolei) ya**
	Πού θά πάρω τό λεωφορεῖο (τρόλλεϋ) γιά . . .;
Does this bus go to . . .?	**pái aftó to leoforío sto**
	Πάει αὐτό τό λεωφορεῖο στό . . .
I want to get off at	**thélo na katévo sto**
	Θέλω νά κατέβω στό . . . .
Do you go near . . .?	**pernáte kondá apó**
	Περνᾶτε κοντά ἀπό . . .;
Is this the stop for . . .?	**íne aftí i stási ya**
	Εἶναι αὐτή στάση γιά . . .;
Please tell me when to get off.	**parakaló péste moo poó prépi na katévo**
	Παρακαλῶ πέστε μου ποὺ πρέπει νά κατέβω.
Do I have to change bus for . . .?	**prépi nalákso leoforío ya na páo sto**
	Πρέπει ν'ἀλλάξω λεωφορεῖο γιά νά πάω στό . . .;

What time is the next bus to . . .?	**ti óra íne to epómeno leoforío ya** *Τί ὥρα εἶναι τό ἐπόμενο λεωφορεῖο γιά . . .;*
*You get off at the next stop.	**tha katévete stin áli stási** *Θά κατέβετε στήν ἄλλη στάση.*
Which bus goes to . . .?	**pyó leoforío pái sto/sti** *Ποιό λεωφορεῖο πάει στό/στή . . .;*
One ticket to the last stop.	**éna isitírio ya to térma** *Ἕνα εἰσιτήριο γιά τό τέρμα.*
How much is it?	**póso káni** *Πόσο κανει;*
How long does it take to get there?	**pósi óra íne i *thia*thromí** *Πόση ὥρα εἶναι ἡ διαδρομή;*
Where is the bus station for . . .?	**poo íne o stathmós leoforíon ya** *Ποῦ εἶναι ὁ σταθμός λεωφορείων γιά . . .;*

By air

There are two airports in Athens very near to each other.
1. The **T*hitikó*** (west) airport, which is used for domestic and international flights by the Olympic Airways *only*.
2. The **Anatolikó** (east) airport which is used by all the foreign airlines.

Olympic Airways operate a particularly comprehensive domestic network (serving most cities and larger islands) which is well worth using if you are short of time.

Tickets and information are available at travel agents, NTOG and Olympic Airlines at 6 Othonos Street, Athens (*ΟΘΩΝΟΣ*), Tel. 9292-444.

Note: Greek air hostesses, airport staff, and booking clerks speak English, so you should not have any language problems.

Note: Airport buses will take you to Sintagma Square (Constitution Square), in Athens.

By ship

The greek islands are as bewitching as the sirens' song, and you, like Odysseus, will find it difficult to resist their pull.

Most shipping offices are in Piraeus (the port of Athens) but tickets may be obtained from most travel agencies in Athens (or other cities).

There are frequent boat services to the islands from Piraeus (and some from Rafina). Several boats a day go to the nearest islands such as Aegina, Poros, Hydra and Spetse. For the further ones, you might have to spend more than twenty-four hours on board.

Most boats are ferry boats which take passengers with or without cars. Some are very fast (the hydrofoil craft) and others stop at many islands before reaching their destination.

Find out how long the journey will take and avoid travelling on public holidays, when the boats may be overbooked. You can always buy tickets in advance. There is a weekly schedule of departures available in English, from the NTOG in Athens and from NTOG abroad.

You can also telephone 451131 or 4113626 for information in English.

Is there a boat for (Naxos) on Sunday?	**éhi plío ya (tin Nákso) tin Kiriakí** *Ἔχει πλοῖο γιά (τήν Νάξο) τήν Κυριακή;*
What other islands does the boat call at?	**se pyá ála nisyà stamatái** *Σέ ποιά ἄλλα νησιά σταματάει;*
How much is the ticket for	**póso káni to isitírio ya** *Πόσο κάνει τό εἰσιτήριο γιά . . . .*
– first class?	**– tin próti thési** *– τήν πρώτη θέση;*
– second class?	**– tin théfteri thési** *– τήν δεύτερη θέση;*

– tourist class?	**– tin tooristikí thési**
	– τήν τουριστική θέση;
– deck?	**– katástroma**
	– κατάστρωμα;
Can I book a cabin with one (two) beds?	**boró naklíso cabína me éna (thío) krevátia**
	Μπορῶ νά κλείσω καμπίνα μ' ἕνα (δύο) κρεββάτια;
I want to travel deck.	**thélo na taksithépso katástroma**
	Θέλω νά ταξιδέψω κατάστρωμα.
Do you have a reduction for children?	**kánete ékptosi ya ta pethyá**
	Κάνετε ἔκπτωση γιά τά παιδιά;
What time does it sail?	**ti óra févghi**
	Τί ὥρα φεύγει;
Where from?	**apó poo**
	Ἀπό ποῦ;
When does it get to . . .?	**póte fthání**
	Πότε φτάνει . . .;
Does it call at . . .?	**stamatái stin**
	Σταματάει στήν . . .;
Can we go ashore?	**boroóme na katevoóme**
	Μπορούμε νά κατεβοῦμε;
For how long?	**ya pósi óra**
	Γιά πόση ὥρα;
Does this ship carry cars?	**metaféri aftokínita aftó to plío**
	Μεταφέρει αὐτοκίνητα αὐτό τό πλοῖο;
Will the sea be rough?	**tháhoome thálassa**
	Θάχουμε θάλασσα;
Where is the agent for the boat ('St Nicholas')?	**poo íne to praktorío ya to plío ('Ayios Nichólas')**
	Ποῦ εἶναι τό πρακτορεῖο γιά τό πλοῖο ('Ἅγιος Νικόλαος');

Taxis

They have meters like London Taxis. There is a flat rate charge upon hire and then a fixed price per kilometre within the Athens area.

Extras: a small additional charge when collecting a passenger from an airport or station; a small charge for every piece of luggage and a supplement is charged between the hours of 12.00 p.m. and 7.00 a.m. A tip is customary.

Are you free?	**íne eléfthero**
	Εἶναι ἐλεύθερο;
I want to go to . . . please.	**thélo na páo sto . . . parakaló**
	Θέλω νά πάω στό . . . παρακαλῶ.
I am in a hurry, could you go faster?	**viázome polí, boríte na páte pyó ghríghora**
	Βιάζομαι πολύ, μπορεῖτε νά πᾶτε πιό γρήγορα;
Stop here.	**stamatíste ethó**
	Σταματῆστε ἐδῶ.
Please wait here for a few minutes.	**parakaló periménete ethó ya lígha leptá**
	Παρακαλῶ περιμένετε ἐδῶ γιά λίγα λεπτά.
Could you bring my luggage inside (upstairs) please?	**boríte na moo férete tis valítses mésa (epáno) parakaló**
	Μπορεῖτε νά μοῦ φέρετε τίς βαλίτσες μέσα (ἐπάνω) παρακαλῶ;
Call me a taxi please.	**moo fonázete éna taxí parakaló**
	Μοῦ φωνάζετε ἕνα ταξί παρακαλῶ.

Your car

Seeing Greece by car is very enjoyable as there is less traffic than at home and the main trunk roads are good.

Here are a few points you might find helpful:
1.   Driving is on the right, overtaking on the left.

2. Traffic coming from the right has priority except on posted main highways.

3. Distances are indicated in kilometres.

4. International Road Signs are used throughout the country and signposts are in Greek and English.

5. Holders of British driving licences do *not* require an international driving licence.

6. Car insurance in Greece is compulsory.

7. Road assistance is given to the foreign motorist by the Automobile and Touring Club of Greece *ΕΛΠΑ* (ELPA) who answers calls when 104 is dialled. Spares, on the spot repairs and towing are part of the service they provide. ELPA (Head Office, 2 Messogion (*ΜΕΣΟΓΕΙΩΝ*) Street, Athens, Tel. 7791-615) also provides information on road conditions, hotels and free legal advice.

8. Special care should be taken when traversing unguarded railway level crossings and during the night when road works, sometimes, are unlighted.

9. Parking is controlled and police can tow away cars causing obstruction or impose fines on the spot. In Athens there are certain parking places reserved for tourists' cars, and indicated by notices.

Foreign car locations in Athens

1.	Tossitsa Street	*ΤΟΣΙΤΣΑ*
2.	Vas. Konstantinou Avenue	*ΛΕΩΦ. ΒΑΣ. ΚΩΝΣΤΑΝΤΙΝΟΥ*
3.	Deligianni Street	*ΔΕΛΗΓΙΑΝΝΗ*
4.	Sina Street (behind the Cathedral)	*ΣΙΝΑ*
5.	Mitropoleos Street	*ΜΗΤΡΟΠΟΛΕΩΣ*
6.	Halkokondili Street	*ΧΑΛΚΟΚΟΝΔΥΑΗ*

7. Kotzia Square	*ΚΟΤΖΙΑ*
8. Xenofondos Street	*ΞΕΝΟΦΩΝΤΟΣ*
9. Koumoundourou Square	*ΠΛ. ΚΟΥΜΟΥΝΔΟΥΡΟΥ*
10. Olgas Avenue	*ΛΕΩΦ. ΟΛΓΑΣ*
11. Areos Street	*ΑΡΕΩΣ*
12. Akadimias Street (behind the University)	*ΑΚΑΔΗΜΙΑΣ*

Servicing and repairs
Service-stations and repair-shops are easy to find in all towns, and repairs are usually done very quickly.

Where is	**poo íne**
	Πού εἶναι . . . .
– the nearest garage?	**– éna garáz et*h*ó kondá**
	– ἕνα γκαράζ ἐδῶ κοντά;
– the motorway for . . .?	**– i ethnikí ot*h*ós ya**
	– ἡ Ἐθνική ὁδός γιά . . .;
Where is the nearest car park?	**poo boró na parkáro et*h*ó kondá**
	Πού μπορῶ νά παρκάρω ἐδῶ κοντά;
Can I park here?	**boró na parkáro et*h*ó**
	Μπορῶ νά παρκάρω ἐδῶ;
What does this . . . mean?	**ti léi**
	Τί λέι . . .;
– notice	**– aftí i pinakít*h*a**
	– αὐτή ἡ πινακίδα
– sign	**– aftó to síma**
	– αὐτό τό σῆμα

At the petrol station

I would like ten litres of standard/ premium petrol.	**thélo théka (10) lítra aplí/ soóper venzíni**
	Θέλω δέκα 10 λίτρα ἁπλῆ/σοῦπερ βενζίνη.
I would like some petrol/oil/water.	**thélo venzíni/lat*h*i/neró**
	Θέλω βενζίνη/λάδι/νερό.

Fill it up.	**na to yemísete**
	Νά τό γεμίσετε.
Please check	**parakaló kitákste**
	Παρακαλῶ κυττάξτε ....
– the oil.	**– to láthi**
	– τό λάδι.
– the water.	**– to neró**
	– τό νερό.
– the battery.	**– tin bataría**
	– τήν μπαταρία.
– the tyre pressure.	**– ta lástiha**
	– τά λάστιχα.
– the spare tyre.	**– tin resérva**
	– τήν ρεζέρβα.
*How much air do you put in?	**póso vázete**
	Πόσο βάζετε;
Please change this tyre.	**parakaló alákste aftó to lástiho**
	Παρακαλῶ ἀλλάξετε αὐτό τό λάστιχο.
Wash the car please.	**plínete to aftokínito parakaló**
	Πλύνετε τό αὐτοκίνητο παρακαλῶ.
Could you fix this?	**boríte na thiorthósete aftó**
	Μπορεῖτε νά διορθώσετε αὐτό;
Do you sell cigarettes/sweets?	**pooláte tsighára/karaméles**
	Πουλᾶτε τσιγάρα/καραμέλες;
Where is the lavatory?	**poo íne i tooaléta**
	Ποῦ εἶναι ἡ τουαλέττα;

At the garage for repairs

Can you help me?	**boríte na me voithísete**
	Μπορεῖτε νά μέ βοηθήσετε;
My car has broken down.	**hálase to aftokínito moo**
	Χάλασε τό αὐτοκίνητό μου.
Can you send a mechanic here?	**boríte na stílete énan mihanikó ethó**
	Μπορεῖτε νά στείλετε ἕναν μηχανικό ἐδῶ;

Can you send a breakdown truck to tow it?

boríte na stílete ena yeranó na pári to aftokínito moo
Μπορεῖτε νά στείλετε ἕνα γερανό νά πάρει τό αὐτοκίνητο μου;

I am near the . . . .

íme kondá sto
Εἶμαι κοντά στό . . . .

My car won't start.

to aftokínito moo *then* pérni bros
Τό αὐτοκίνητό μου δέν παίρνει μπρός.

I've run out of petrol.

***then* ého venzíni**
Δέν ἔχω βενζίνη.

I think there is something wrong with . . . .

nomízo óti éhi vlávi
Νομίζω ὅτι ἔχει βλάβη . . . .

– the carburettor.

– to karbiratér
– τό καρμπυρατέρ.

– the hand-brake.

– to hirófreno
– τό χειρόφρενο.

– the brakes.

– ta fréna
– τα φρένα.

– the clutch.

– to ambrayáz (simpléktis)
– τό ἀμπραγιάζ (συμπλέκτης).

– the horn.

– to klákson
– τό κλάξον.

– the gears.

– i tahítites
– οἱ ταχύτητες.

– the accelerator.

– to gázi
– τό γκάζι.

– the ignition.

– i míza
– ἡ μίζα.

– the lights.

– ta fóta
– τά φῶτα.

The fan-belt is broken.

i loorítha too anemistíra kopike
Ἡ λουρίδα τοῦ ἀνεμιστῆρα κόπηκε.

The windscreen-wipers aren't working.

i ialokatharistíres *then* thoolévoon
Οἱ ὑαλοκαθαριστῆρες δέν δουλεύουν.

The steering wheel is vibrating.	**to timóni trémi**
	Τό τιμόνι 'τρέμει.
The radiator is leaking.	**to psighío tréhi**
	Τό ψυγεῖο τρέχει.
The engine is overheating.	**i mihaní zesténete polí (iperthérménete).**
	Ἡ μηχανή ζεσταίνεται πολύ (ὑπερθερμαίνετ).
I have got a puncture.	**aftó to lástiho trípise**
	Αὐτό τό λάστιχο τρύπησε.
The battery is flat, could you charge it?	**i bataría íne áthia, boríte na tin yemísete**
	Ἡ μπαταρία εἶναι ἄδεια, μπορεῖτε νά τήν γεμίσετε;
The plug is dirty.	**to boozí théli kathárisma**
	Τό μπουζί θέλει καθάρισμα.
There is a smell of petrol/rubber.	**mirízi venzíni/lástiho**
	Μυρίζει βενζίνη/λάστιχο.
There is a petrol/oil/water leak.	**tréhi i venzíni/to láthi/to neró**
	Τρέχει ἡ βενζίνη/τό λάδι/τό νερό.
There is a noise.	**káni éna thórivo**
	Κάνει ἕνα θόρυβο.
How long will it take to repair?	**póso keró tha sas pári i episkeví**
	Πόσο καιρό θά σᾶς πάρει ἡ ἐπισκευή;
What's it going to cost?	**ti tha stihísi**
	Τί θά στοιχίσει;
*We haven't the right spares.	***th*én éhoome ta katálila andalaktiká**
	Δέν ἔχομε τά κατάλληλα ἀνταλλακτικά.
*We have to order the spares.	**prépi na paraghíloome ta andalaktiká**
	Πρέπει νά παραγγείλουμε τά ἀνταλλακτικά.
Have you got	**éhete**
	Ἔχετε . . . .

– another tyre?	– **éna lástiho**
	– ἕνα λάστιχο;
– a can of petrol?	– **éna bitóni me venzíni**
	– ἕνα μπιτόνι μέ βενζίνη;
– a can of oil?	– **éna kootí lá*th*i mihanís**
	– ἕνα κουτί λάδι μηχανῆς;
– a can of brake fluid?	– **ighró ya ta fréna**
	– ὑγρό γιά τά φρένα;
– a jack?	– **éna ghrílo**
	– ἕνα γρύλλο;
– pressure gauge?	– **piesómetro ya ta lástiha**
	– πιεσόμετρο γιά τά λάστιχα;

Hiring a car

I'd like to hire a car, please.	**thélo na nikyáso éna aftokínito parakaló**
	Θέλω νά νοικιάσω ἕνα αὐτοκίνητο παρακαλῶ.
With a driver.	**me sofér**
	Μέ σωφέρ.
Without a driver.	**horís sofér**
	Χωρίς σωφέρ.
The smallest/biggest you have.	**to meghalítero/mikrótero poo éhete**
	Τό μεγαλύτερο/μικρότερο πού ἔχετε.
A mini.	**éna míni**
	Ἕωα μίνι.
A two/four door.	**me *th*ío/téseris pórtes**
	Μέ δύο/τέσσερεις πόρτες.
A sports car.	**éna aftokínito spor**
	Ἕνα αὐτοκίνητο σπόρ.
A convertible.	**éna convertíbl (aniktó)**
	Ἕνα κονβερτίμπλ (ἀνοικτό).
An automatic.	**aftómato**
	Αὐτόματο.

For . . . days.	**ya . . . méres** *Γιά . . . μέρες.*
for one/two weeks.	**ya mía/thío evthomáth-(a) (-es)** *Γιά μιά/δύο ἑβδομάδ(-α) (-ες).*
Do you charge per kilometre?	**to hreónete me to hiliómetro** *Τό χρεώνετε μέ τό* *χιλιόμετρο;*
What is the charge per day/week/ hour?	**póso káni ya mía méra/evthomátha** **/óra** *Πόσο κάνει γιά μιά μέρα/ἑβδομάδα/* *ὥρα;*
Does that include petrol?	**i timí éhi mésa ke tin venzíni** *Ἡ τιμή ἔχει μέσα καί τήν βενζίνη;*
Does this include insurance (full)?	**i timí éhi mésa ke tin ásfália (miktí)** *Ἡ τιμή ἔχει μέσα καί τήν ἀσφάλεια* *(μικτή);*
Can I see the insurance certificate please?	**boró na tho to simvóleo tis asfálías** **parakaló** *Μπορῶ νά δῶ τό συμβόλαιο τῆς* *ἀσφάλειας παρακαλῶ;*
Can I return it in a different town?	**boró na to epistrépso sáli póli** *Μπορῶ νά τό ἐπιστρέψω σ'ἄλλη* *πόλη;*
Must I bring it back here?	**prépi na to epistrépso ethó** *Πρέπει νά τό ἐπιστρέψω ἐδῶ;*
Have you got an office in . . .?	**éhete ghrafío sto/stin** *Ἔχετε γραφεῖο στό/στήν . . .;*
Is there a deposit?	**hreázete prokatavolí** *Χρειάζεται προκαταβολή;*
Can I see the car please?	**boró na tho to aftokínito parakaló** *Μπορῶ νά δῶ τό αὐτοκίνητο* *παρακαλῶ;*

WRITTEN ROAD SIGNS

ΟΔΗΓΗΤΕ ΑΡΓΑ	Drive slowly
ΠΡΟΣΟΧΗ	Drive carefully

ΑΡΓΑ	SLOW
STOP	STOP
ΣΧΟΛΕΙΟΝ	School
ΟΔΙΚΑ :ΕΡΓΑ or ΔΗΜΟΣΙΑ ΕΡΓΑ	Roadworks
ΠΑΡΑΚΑΜΠΤΗΡΙΟΣ	Diversion
ΕΘΝΙΚΗ ΟΔΟΣ	Motorway
ΣΙΔΗΡΟΔΡΟΜΙΚΗ ΔΙΑΒΑΣΙΣ	Level crossing
ΜΟΝΟΔΡΟΜΟΣ	One-way street
ΑΠΑΓΟΡΕΥΕΤΑΙ Η ΣΤΑΘΜΕΥΣΙΣ	No parking
ΙΔΙΩΤΙΚΟΣ ΔΡΟΜΟΣ	Private road
ΚΙΝΔΥΝΟΣ	Danger
ΑΔΙΕΞΟΔΟΣ	No through road

Asking the way and directions

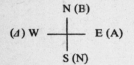

North	**o vorás**	*Βορρᾶς*
South	**o nótos**	*Νότος*
East	**i anatolí**	*'Ανατολή*
West	**i thísi**	*Δύση*

Left	**aristerá** *ἀριστερά*
Right	**theksiá** *δεξιά*

Excuse me.	**me sinhoríte**
	Μέ συγχωρεῖτε.
Can you tell me the way to . . .?	**pos tha páo sto**
	Πῶς θά πάω στό . . .ʹ
Where is?	**poo íne**
	Ποῦ εἶναι;
Is this the way to . . . ?	**aftós íne o thrómos ya**
	Αὐτός εἶναι ὁ δρόμος γιά . . .;
How far is it, if I walk it?	**póso makriá íne me ta póthya**
	Πόσο μακριά εἶναι μέ τά πόδια;

Can I take a bus there?	**éhi leoforío ya ekí**
	Ἔχει λεωφορεῖο γιά ἐκεῖ;
Where is it on this map?	**poo íne ston hárti**
	Ποῦ εἶναι στόν χάρτη;
Where am I, on this map?	**poo íme eghó ston hárti**
	Ποῦ εἶμαι ἐγώ, στόν χάρτη;
Where does this road lead to?	**poo piyéni aftós o thrómos**
	Ποῦ πηγαίνει αὐτός ὁ δρόμος;
*Go back.	**yiríste píso**
	Γυρίστε πίσω.
*Carry straight on.	**piyénete ísya**
	Πηγαίνετε ἴσια.
*Turn right.	**strípste theksiá**
	Στρίψτε δεξιά.
*Turn left.	**strípste aristerá**
	Στρίψτε ἀριστερά.
*Take the	**párte**
	Πᾶρτε . . . .
– first road.	**– ton próto thrómo**
	– τόν πρῶτο δρόμο.
– second road.	**– ton théftero thrómo**
	– τόν δεύτερο δρόμο.
– third road.	**– ton tríto thrómo**
	– τόν τρίτο δρόμο.
On the right.	**theksiá**
	δεξιά.
On the left.	**aristerà**
	ἀριστερά
*Turn right/left at the	**strípste theksià/aristerà**
	Στρίψτε δεξιά/ἀριστερά . . . .
– traffic lights.	**– sta fóta**
	– στά φῶτα.
– cross-roads.	**– sto stavrothrómi**
	– στό σταυροδρόμι.
– main road.	**– ston kírio thrómo**
	– στόν κύριο δρόμο.

– cinema.

— sto cinemà
— *στό σινεμά.*

Then ask again.

ke ksanarotíste
Καί ξαναρωτῆστε.

*You are on the wrong road.

éhete pári láthos *th*rómo
Ἔχετε πάρει λάθος δρόμο.

*Cross the road.

piyénete apénandi
Πηγαίνετε ἀπέναντι.

*It is right here.

íne e*th*ó
Εἶναι ἐδῶ.

*It is only a short way from here.

íne polí kondá
Εἶναι πολύ κοντά.

*It is a long way.

íne polí makriá
Εἶναι πολύ μακρυά.

*An hour's walk.

mía óra me ta pó*th*ya
Μιά ὥρα μέ τά πόδια.

*An hour's drive.

mía óra me to aftokínito
Μιά ὥρα μέ τό αὐτοκίνητο.

*Five kilometres.

pénde hilyómetra
Πέντε χιλιόμετρα.

*It's about two blocks from here.

*th*ío tetrághona parakáto
Δύο τετράγωνα παρακάτω.

Shopping

Shops and shopkeepers

The words in capital Greek letters are the written signs you will see outside the shops. The words in phonetics, are the colloquial terms used when referring to the shops or to the shopkeepers.

Opening hours are generally from 8 a.m. to 1.30 p.m. and from 5 p.m. to 8 p.m. or from 8 a.m. to 3 p.m. depending on the type of shop and on the day of the week and whether it is summer or winter.

Where is the . . .?	**poo íne** *Πού είναι . . .;*
baker	**o foórnos** *ὁ φοῦρνος* *(ΑΡΤΟΠΩΛΕΙΟΝ)*
bank	**i trápeza** *ἡ τράπεζα* *(ΤΡΑΠΕΖΑ)*
barber	**to koorío** *τό κουρεῖο* *(ΚΟΥΡΕΙΟΝ)*
bookshop	**to vivliopolío** *τό βιβλιοπωλεῖο* *(ΒΙΒΛΙΟΠΩΛΕΙΟΝ)*
butcher	**o hasápis** *ὁ χασάπης* *(ΚΡΕΟΠΩΛΕΙΟΝ)*
cake-shop	**to zaharoplastío** *τό* *ζαχαροπλαστεῖο* *(ΖΑΧΑΡΟΠΛΑΣΤΕΙΟΝ)*
chemist	**to farmakío** *τό φαρμακεῖο* *(ΦΑΡΜΑΚΕΙΟΝ)*
dairy shop	**to ghalaktopolío** *τό* *γαλακτοπωλεῖο* *(ΓΑΛΑΚΤΟΠΩΛΕΙΟΝ)*

draper	**to emborikó** *τό ἐμπορικό* (ΕΜΠΟΡΙΚΟΝ)
dry-cleaner	**to katharistírio** *τό καθαριστήριο* (ΚΑΘΑΡΙΣΤΗΡΙΟΝ)
electrical goods	**ta ilektriká ííħi** *τὰ ἠλεκτρικά εἴδη* (ΗΛΕΚΤΡΙΚΑ ΕΙΔΗ)
electrician	**o ilektrológhos** *ὁ ἠλεκτρολόγος*
fishmonger	**o psarás** *ὁ ψαρᾶς* (ΙΧΘΥΟΠΩΛΕΙΟΝ)
florist	**to anthopolíon** *τό ἀνθοπωλεῖον* (ΑΝΘΟΠΩΛΕΙΟΝ)
furrier	**to katástima ghoonarikón** *τό κατάστημα γουναρικῶν* (ΚΑΤΑΣΤΗΜΑ ΓΟΥΝΑΡΙΚΩΝ)
greengrocer	**o manávis** *ὁ μανάβης* (ΟΠΩΡΟΠΩΛΕΙΟΝ)
grocer	**o bakális** *ὁ μπακάλης* (ΠΑΝΤΟΠΩΛΕΙΟΝ)
hairdresser	**to komotírio** *τό κομμωτήριο* (ΚΟΜΜΩΤΗΡΙΟΝ)
jeweller	**to kosmimatopolío** *τό κοσμηματοπωλεῖο* (ΚΟΣΜΗΜΑΤΟΠΩΛΕΙΟΝ)
Kiosk	**to períptero** *τό περίπτερο* (ΠΕΡΙΠΤΕΡΟΝ)
laundry	**to plindírio** *τό πλυντήριο* (ΠΛΥΝΤΗΡΙΟΝ)
market	**i aghorá** *ἡ ἀγορά* (ΑΓΟΡΑ)
photographer	**to fotoghrafío** *τό φωτογραφεῖο* (ΦΩΤΟΓΡΑΦΕΙΟΝ)
police station	**i astinomía** *ἡ ἀστυνομία* (ΑΣΤΥΜΟΜΙΑ)
post-office	**to tahiťhromío** *τό ταχυδρομεῖο* (ΤΑΧΥΔΡΟΜΕΙΟ)
shoemaker (repairs)	**o tsanghláris** *ὁ τσαγκάρης*

shoe-shop	**to katástima ya papoótsia** *τό κατάστημα γιά παπούτσια (ΥΠΟΔΗΜΑΤΟΠΟΙΕΙΟΝ)*
shop (small)	**to maghazí** *τό μαγαζί*
shop (big)	**to katástima** *τό κατάστημα*
souvenir shop	**katastima ya soovenir** *τό κατάστημα γιά σουβενίρ (ΣΟΥΒΕΝΙΡ)*
stationer	**to hartopolío** *τό χαρτοπωλείο (ΧΑΡΤΟΠΩΛΕΙΟΝ)*
supermarket	**i 'supermarket'** *ἡ σουπερμάρκετ (ΣΟΥΠΕΡΜΑΡΚΕΤ)*
tobacconist	**tó kapnopolío** *τό καπνοπωλεῖο (ΕΙΔΗ ΚΑΠΝΙΣΤΩΝ)*
tailor	**o ráftis** *ὁ ράφτυς (ΡΑΦΕΙΟΝ)*
travel agent	**to praktoríon taksíthion** *τό πρακτορεῖον ταξιδιον (ΠΡΑΚΤΟΡΕΙΟΝ ΤΑΞΙΔΙΩΝ)*

In a food shop

Please have you got . . .?	**parakaló éhete** *Παρακαλῶ ἔχετε . . . .*
– beer	**– bíra** *– μπίρα*
– biscuits	**– biskóta** *– μπισκότα*
– bread (brown, white)	**– psomí (mávro, áspro)** *– ψωμί (μαῦρο, ἄσπρο)*
– butter (European, local)	**– voótiro (evropaikó, dópyo)** *– βούτυρο (εὐρωπαϊκό, ντόπιο)*
– cheese	**– tirí** *– τυρί*
– a chocolate (plain, milk)	**– sokoláta (skéti, ghálaktos)** *– σοκολάτα (σκέτη, γάλακτος)*

– coffee
– crackers
– crisps
– eggs
– ice-cream
– lemonade (bottle of)
– luncheon meat (ham)
– milk
– mineral water
– mustard
– olives (black, green)
– orange drink
– pepper
– rice
– salami
– salt
– sausages
– sugar

– **kafé**
– *καφέ*
– **krakerákia**
– *κρακεράκια*
– **tsíps**
– *τσίπς*
– **avghá**
– *αὐγά*
– **paghotó**
– *παγωτό*
– **éna bookáli lemonátha**
– *ἕνα μπουκάλι λεμονάδα*
– **zambón**
– *ζαμπόν*
– **ghála**
– *γάλα*
– **botilyarisméno nero**
– *μποτιλιαρισμένο νερό*
– **moostártha**
– *μουστάρδα*
– **elyés (mávres, prásines)**
– *ἐλιές, (μαῦρες, πράσινες)*
– **portokalátha**
– *πορτοκαλάδα*
– **pipéri**
– *πιπέρι*
– **rízi**
– *ρύζι*
– **salámi**
– *σαλάμι*
– **aláti**
– *ἀλάτι*
– **lookánika**
– *λουκάνικα*
– **záhari**
– *ζάχαρι*

– sweets	– **karaméles**
	– *καραμέλλες*
– tea	– **tsái**
	– *τσάϊ*
– a tin of tomatoes	– **éna kootí domátes**
	– *ἕνα κουτί ντομάτες*
– wine	– **krasí**
	– *κρασί*
– a bottle of	– **éna bookáli**
	– *ἕνα μπουκάλι* . . . .
– a tin (can) of	– **mía konsérva**
	– *μιά κονσέρβα* . . . .
I want	**thélo**
	Θέλω . . . .
– a kilo	– **éna kiló**
	– *ἕνα κιλό*
– half a kilo	– **misó kiló**
	– *μισό κιλό*
– quarter of a kilo	– **éna tétarto**
	– *ἕνα τέταρτο*
Have you got a carrier bag please?	**éhete mía sakoóla parakaló**
	Ἔχετε μιά σακκούλα, παρακαλῶ;
Where do they sell . . .?	**poo pooláne**
	Ποῦ πουλᾶνε . . .;

Note: For more items, see 'Food' section.

The Kiosk

The Kiosks (**períptero**) to be found every hundred yards or so, along main streets, are always open from morning till late at night. It is quite incredible what one is able to find in them! This is where you buy your stamps, make your calls, ask the way, buy your cigarettes, sweets, newspapers, aspirins, batteries, postcards, almost anything you might need.

Do you have a/some	**éhete**
	Ἔχετε . . . .
– aspirins?	**– aspirínes**
	– ἀσπιρίνες;
– ball-point pen?	**– éna bik**
	– ἕνα μπίκ;
– envelopes (air mail)?	**– fakéloos (aeroporikoós)**
	– φακέλλους (ἀεροπορικούς);
– hair grips?	**– stekákya**
	– στεκάκια;
– hair pins?	**– foorkétes**
	– φουρκέττες;
– newspaper?	**– mia efimerítha**
	– μια ἐφημερίδα;
(American)	**(amerikanikí)**
	(Ἀμερικανική)
(English)	**(anglikí)**
	(Ἀγγλική)
(French)	**(ghalikí)**
	(Γαλλική)
(German)	**(yermanikí)**
	(Γερμανική)
– pencil?	**– éna molívi**
	– ενα μολύβι;
– post-cards?	**– kártes**
	– κάρτες;
– razor-blades?	**– ksirafákya**
	– ξυραφάκια;
– safety-pins?	**– paramánes**
	– παραμάνες;
– sweets?	**– karaméles**
	– καραμέλες;
– writing-pad?	**– éna blok**
	– ἕνα μπλόκ;

Kiosks also have telephones for the public (usually red).

ΤΗΛΕΦΩΝΟ ΔΙΑ ΤΟ ΚΟΙΝΟ	public telephone
ΕΔΩ ΤΗΛΕΦΩΝΕΙΤΕ	public telephone here

At the kiosk or at the tobacconist
You might develop a liking for Greek cigarettes (like retsina, these are another acquired taste). These are some of the most usual brands: **Aroma, Assos, Carelia, Old Navy, Pallas, Papastratos I** etc.

Do you have a/some	**éhete**
	Ἔχετε . . . .
– cigars?	**– poóra**
	– ποῦρα;
– cigarettes?	**– tsighára**
	– τσιγάρα;
(tipped)	**(me fíltro)**
	(μέ φίλτρο)
(untipped)	**(horís fíltro)**
	(χωρίς φίλτρο)
– flints?	**– pétres ya anaptíra**
	– πέτρες γιά ἀναπτῆρα;
– lighter?	**– énan anaptíra**
	– ἕναν ἀναπτῆρα;
– lighter fuel/gas?	**– venzíni/aério ya anaptíra**
	– βενζίνη/ἀέριο γιά ἀναπτῆρα;
– matches?	**– spírta**
	– σπίρτα;
– pipe?	**– mía pípa**
	– μιά πίπα;
– pipe cleaners?	**– katharistés pípas**
	– καθαριστές πίπας;
– tobacco?	**– kapnó ya pípa**
	– καπνό γιά πίπα;
I would like	**tha íthela**
	Θά ἤθελα . . . .
– American cigarettes.	**– amerikánika tsighára**
	– ἀμερικάνικα τσιγάρα.
– English cigarettes.	**– englézika tsighára**
	– ἐγγλέζικα τσιγάρα.
– Greek cigarettes.	**– elinikà tsighára**
	– ἑλληνικά τσιγάρα.

– menthol cigarettes.

  – **tsighára méndas**
  – *τσιγάρα μέντας.*

– strong cigarettes.

  – **varyá tsighára**
  – *βαρειά τσιγάρα.*

– very mild cigarettes.

  – **polí elafrá tsighára**
  – *πολύ ἐλαφρά τσιγάρα.*

Smoking

Would you like a cigarette?

thélete éna tsigháro
Θέλετε ἕνα τσιγάρο;

No, thanks, I don't smoke.

óhi efharistó then kapnízo
Ὄχι εὐχαριστῶ, δέν καπνίζω.

Yes, thank you.

ne efharistó
Ναί, εὐχαριστῶ.

Books and stationery

Do you sell American/English newspapers?

éhete Amerikanikés/Anglikés efimeríthes
Ἔχετε Ἀμερικανικές/Ἀγγλικές ἐφημερίδες;

Can you order this newspaper/ magazine for me?

boríte na moo parangílete aftín tin efimerítha/aftó to periothikó
Μπορεῖτε νά μοῦ παραγγείλετε αὐτήν τήν ἐφημερίδα/αὐτό τό περιοδικό;

I would like it every day/once a week.

tha to íthela káthe méra/káthe evthomátha
Θά τό ἤθελα κάθε μέρα/κάθε ἑβδομάδα.

How much will it cost?

póso tha kostísi
Πόσο θά κοστίσει;

Do you have English books?

éhete angliká vivlía
Ἔχετε ἀγγλικά βιβλία;

Do you have Greek books translated into English?

éhete eliniká vivlía se anglikí metáfrasi
Ἔχετε ἑλληνικά βιβλία σέ ἀγγλική μετάφραση;

Do you have the Seferis/Kavafis poems in English?	**éhete ta piímata too Seféri/too Kaváfi st Angliká**
	Έχετε τά ποιήματα τοῦ Σεφέρη/τοῦ Καβάφη στ ἀγγλικά;

Note: Athens News, Athens Mirror are English language newspapers with local and international news.

Do you have a/some	**éhete**
	Έχετε . . . .
– biro?	**– éna bic**
	– ἕνα μπίκ;
– book?	**– éna vivlío**
	– ἕνα βιβλίο;
– crayons?	**– krayiónya**
	– κραγιόνια;
– Sellotape?	**– 'cellotape'**
	– σελοτέϊπ;
– dictionary?	**– éna leksikó**
	– ἕνα λεξικό;
– envelopes?	**– fakéloos**
	– φακέλλους;
– glue?	**– kóla**
	– κόλλα;
– guide book?	**– éna tooristikó othighó**
	– ἕνα τουριστικό ὁδηγό;
– ink?	**– meláni**
	– μελάνι;
– labels?	**– tikétes**
	– τικέττες;
– magazines?	**– periothiká**
	– περιοδικά;
– map?	**– énan hárti**
	– ἕναν χάρτη;
– map of this town/area?	**– éna hárti aftís tis pólis/tis periohís**
	– ἕνα χάρτη αὐτῆς τῆς πόλης/τῆς περιοχῆς;

– newspapers?
                                 – **efimerí*th*es**
                                 – *ἐφημερίδες;*

– note paper?
                                 – **éna block**
                                 – *ἕνα μπλόκ;*

– pen?
                                 – **éna stiló**
                                 – *ἕνα στυλό;*

– pencil?
                                 – **éna molívi**
                                 – *ἕνα μολύβι;*

– pencil sharpener?
                                 – **mía ksístra**
                                 – *μιά ξύστρα;*

– post-cards?
                                 – **kártes**
                                 – *κάρτες;*

– road map?
                                 – **énan o*th*ikó hárti**
                                 – *ἕναν ὀδικό χάρτη;*

– rubber?
                                 – **mía ghóma**
                                 – *μία γόμα;*

– rubber bands?
                                 – **lastihákya**
                                 – *λαστιχάκια;*

– string?
                                 – **spángo**
                                 – *σπάγγο;*

– wrapping paper?
                                 – **hartí peritilíghmatos**
                                 – *χαρτί περιτυλίγματος;*

At the chemist

Please give me a/some . . . .
                                 parakaló moo *th*ínete
                                 Παρακαλῶ μοῦ δίνετε . . . .

– antiseptic cream.
                                 – **mía antisiptikí alifí**
                                 – *μιά ἀντισηπτική ἀλοιφή.*

– aspirins.
                                 – **aspirínes**
                                 – *ἀσπιρίνες.*

– bandage.
                                 – **énan epí*th*esmo**
                                 – *ἕναν ἐπίδεσμο.*

– band-aids.
                                 – **hansaplást**
                                 – *χανσαπλάστ.*

– contraceptive pills.
                                 – **antisiliptiká hápya**
                                 – *ἀντισυλληπτικά χάπια.*

– corn-plaster.

  – **tsiróta ya káloos**
  – *τσιρότα γιά κάλους.*

– cotton-wool.

  – **babáki**
  – *μπαμπάκι.*

– cough-lozenges

  – **pastílies ya ton víha**
  – *παστίλιες γιά τόν βῆχα.*

– disinfectant.

  – **apolimantikó**
  – *ἀπολυμαντικό.*

– elastoplast.

  – **lefkoplásti**
  – *λευκοπλάστη.*

– laxative.

  – **kathartikó**
  – *καθαρτικό.*

– sanitary towels.

  – **petsétes iyías**
  – *πετσέτες ὑγείας.*

– sedative pills.

  – **iremistiká hápya**
  – *ἠρεμιστικά χάπια.*

– sleeping pills.

  – **ipnotiká hápya**
  – *ὑπνωτικά χάπια.*

– stomach pills.

  – **hápya ya to stomáhi**
  – *Χάπια γιά τό στομάχι.*

– tampax.

  – **'támpax'**
  – *τάμπαξ.*

– thermometer.

  – **éna thermómetro**
  – *ἕνα θερμόμετρο.*

– throat-lozenges.

  – **pastílies ya ton lemó**
  – *παστίλιες γιά τόν λαιμό.*

– vitamin pills.

  – **vitamínes**
  – *βιταμίνες.*

Could you give me something
  for . . . .

boríte na moo *th*ósete káti ya
*Μπορεῖτε νά μοῦ δώσετε κάτι
  γιά . . . .*

– blistered feet.

  – **ta pó*th*ya moo poo éhoon
    fooskáles**
  – *τά πόδια μου πού ἔχουν
    φουσκάλες.*

– diarrhoea.

  – ***th*iária**
  – *διάρροια.*

– indigestion

 – **thispepsía**
 – δυσπεψία.

– insect bites.

 – **ta tsimbímata apó éndoma**
 – τά τσιμπήματα ἀπό ἔντομα.

– sore throat.

 – **ponólemo**
 – πονόλαιμο.

– sunburn.

 – **éngavma ilíoo**
 – ἔγκαυμα ἡλίου.

– travel sickness

 – **naftía**
 – ναυτία.

Can you make up this
 prescription?

**boríte na moo kánete aftí tin
 sintayí**

*Μπορεῖτε νά μοῦ κάνετε αὐτή τήν
 συνταγή;*

ΔΗΑΗΤΗΡΙΟΝ

POISON

*ΔΙΑ ΕΞΩΤΕΡΙΚΕΝ ΧΡΗΣΗ
 ΜΟΝΟΝ*

For external use only

ΣΥΝΤΑΓΑΙ

Prescriptions

ΚΑΤΟΛ (a green oil which burns
 during the night and the smoke
 repels insects).

KATOL

Cosmetics

Do you have a some . . . .

éhete
Ἔχετε . . . .

– cologne.

 – **kolónia**
 – κολώνια.

– cream for . . . .

 – **mía kréma ya**
 – μιά κρέμα γιά . . . .

 the face.

  to prósopo
  τό πρόσωπο.

 the hands.

  ta hérya
  τά χέρια.

 body.

  to sóma
  τό σῶμα.

 lips.

  ta hílya
  τά χείλια.

the day.	**tin méra**
	τήν μέρα.
the night.	**tin níkta**
	τήν νύκτα.
– deodorant.	**– aposmitikó (deodorant)**
	– ἀποσμητικό. (ντιοντοραντ)
– kleenex.	**– klínex**
	– κλινέξ.
– lipstick.	**– krayón**
	– κραγιόν.
– a lotion.	**– mía losión**
	– μιά λοσιόν.
– nail-file.	**– líma ya ta níhya**
	– λίμα γιά τά νύχια.
– shampoo.	**– éna sampooàn**
	– ἔνα σαμπουάν.
– soap.	**– sapoóni**
	– σαπούνι.
– sun-tan cream.	**– mía kréma ya ton ílio**
	– μιά κρέμα γιά τόν ἥλιο.
– sun-tan oil.	**– éna láthi ya ton ílio**
	– ἔνα λάδι γιά τόν ἥλιο.
– talcum powder.	**– talk**
	– τάλκ.
– tissues.	**– hartomándila**
	– χαρτομάνδηλα.
– toilet-paper.	**– hartí tooalétas**
	– χαρτί τουαλέττας.
– tooth-brush.	**– othondóvoortsa**
	– ὀδοντόβουρτσα.
– tooth-paste.	**– othondópasta**
	– ὀδοντόπαστα.
– tweezers.	**– tsimbithàki ya ta fríthya**
	– τσιμπιδάκι γιά τά φρύδια.
– after-shave lotion.	**– mía losión ya metá to ksírisma**
	– μιά λοσιόν γιά μετά τό ξύρισμα.
– razor.	**– mía ksiristikí mihaní**
	– μιά ξυριστική μηχανή.

– razor-blades.	– **ksirafákya**
	– *ξυραφάκια.*
– shaving-cream.	– **mía kréma ksirísmatos**
	– *μιά κρέμα ξυρίσματος.*
– shaving-soap.	– **éna sapoóni ksirísmatos**
	– *ἕνα σαπούνι ξυρίσματος.*

Photography

I'd like . . . please.	**parakaló thélo**
	Παρακλαῶ θέλω . . .
– a film for my camera	– **éna film ya tin mihaní moo**
	– *ἕνα φίλμ γιά τήν μηχανή μου.*
– black and white film	– **mavróaspro film**
	– *μαυρόασπρο φίλμ.*
– colour film	– **énhromo film**
	– *ἔγχρωμο φίλμ.*
– a colour slide film	– **énhromo film ya slídes**
	– *ἔγχρωμο φίλμ γιά σλάϊντς.*
– an 8 mm/35 mm	– **ton októ/ton triánda-pénde hiliostón**
	– *τῶν ὀκτώ/τῶν τριάντα πέντε χιλιοστῶν.*
– with 20/36 exposures	– **me íkosi/me triándaéksi fotografíes**
	– *μέ εἴκοσι/μέ τριάντα ἕξη φωτογραφίες.*
Would you put the film in the camera please?	**moo vázete to film stin mihaní moo sas parakaló**
	Μοῦ βάζετε τό φίλμ στήν μηχανή μου, σᾶς παρακαλῶ;
Do you have flashbulbs?	**éhete flas (ghlombákia)**
	Ἔχετε φλάς; (γλομπάκια)
Will you develop this film please?	**boríte na emfanísete aftó to film parakaló**
	Μπορεῖτε νά ἐμφανίσετε αὐτό τό φίλμ παρακαλῶ;

How much does it cost to develop this film?	**póso kostízi i emphánisi** *Πόσο κοστίζει ἡ ἐμφάνιση;*
I'd like (four) prints of this negative.	**thélo (téseres) fotoghrafíes apó aftó to arnitikó** *Θέλω (τέσσερες) φωτογραφίες ἀπό αὐτό τό ἀρνητικό.*
With a glossy/matt finish.	**se yalisteró/mat hartí** *σέ γυαλιστερό/μάτ χαρτί.*
Will you enlarge this please?	**boríte na meyethínete aftó parakaló** *Μπορεῖτε νά μεγεθύνετε αὐτό παρακαλῶ;*
When will they be ready?	**póte tha íne étima** *Πότε θά εἶναι ἔτοιμα;*
Can you repair my camera?	**boríte na moo ftyáksete tin mihaní moo** *Μπορεῖτε νά μού φτιάξετε τήν μηχανή μου;*
Please would you take out the film?	**moo vgházete to film apó tin mihaní moo, parakaló** *Μοῦ βγάζετε τό φίλμ ἀπό τήν μηχανή μου, παρακαλῶ;*
The film is stuck.	**to film éhi blehtí** *Τό φίλμ ἔχει μπλεχτεῖ.*

Clothes and accessories

I'd like a/some	**tha íthela** *Θά ἤθελα . . . .*
– bathing cap.	**– mía skoófya ya to bányo** *– μιά σκούφια γιά τό μπάνιο.*
– bathing-suit.	**– éna mayió** *– ἕνα μαγιό.*
– bathing trunks.	**– ena mayió** *– ἕνα μαγιό.*
– blouse.	**– mía bloóza** *– μιά μπλούζα.*

– bras.
 – **éna sootién**
 – ἔνα σουτιέν.

– cardigan (knitted).
 – **mía plékti zakéta**
 – μιά πλεκτή ζακέτα.

– coat.
 – **éna paltó**
 – ἔνα παλτό.

– dress.
 – **éna foostáni**
 – ἔνα φουστάνι.

– dressing-gown.
 – **mía rómba**
 – μιά ρόμπα.

– fur.
 – **mía ghoóna**
 – μιά γούνα.

– gloves.
 – **ghándia**
 – γάντια.

– handkerchief.
 – **éna mandíli**
 – ἔνα μαντῆλι.

– hat.
 – **éna kapélo**
 – ἔνα καπέλλο.

– hat (straw).
 – **éna psáthino kapélo**
 – ἔνα ψάθινο καπέλλο.

– jacket.
 – **mía zakéta**
 – μιά ζακέτα.

– jeans.
 – **jeans (dzins)**
 – τζήνς.

– lingerie.
 – **esórooha**
 – ἐσώρρουχα.

– nightdress.
 – **éna niktikó**
 – ἔνα νυκτικό.

– panties.
 – **kilótes**
 – κυλότες.

– petticoat.
 – **mía combinezón**
 – μιά κομπιναιζόν.

– pullover.
 – **éna poolóver**
 – ἔνα πουλόβερ.

– pyjamas.
 – **pizámes**
 – πυτζάμες.

– raincoat.	– **éna at*h*iávroho**
	– ἔνα ἀδιάβροχο.
– scarf.	– **éna kaskól**
	– ἔνα κασκόλ.
– shirt.	– **éna pookàmiso**
	– ἔνα πουκάμισο.
– shorts.	– **éna sórt**
	– ἔνα σόρτ.
– skirt.	– **mía foósta**
	– μιά φούστα.
– slacks.	– **éna pandelóni**
	– ἔνα παντελόνι.
– slippers.	– **pandófles**
	– Παντόφλες.
– socks.	– **káltses (kondés)**
	– κάλτσες (κοντές).
– stockings.	– **káltses yinekíes**
	– κάλτσες (γυναικεῖες).
– suit (men).	– **éna koostoómi**
	– ἔνα κουστούμι.
– suit (women).	– **éna tayiér**
	– ἔνα ταγιέρ.
– tee-shirt.	– **éna 'tee shirt'**
	– ἔνα τι-σέρτ.
– tie.	– **mía ghraváta**
	– μιά γραβάτα.
– tights.	– **kalsón**
	– καλσόν.
– trousers (men).	– **éna pandelóni ant*h*rikó**
	– ἔνα παντελόνι ἀνδρικό.
– underpants (men).	– **éna sóvrako**
	– ἔνα σώβρακο.
– waistcoat.	– **éna yiléko**
	– ἔνα γιλέκο.
*Can I help you?	**ti thélete na sas *th*ikso**
	Τί θέλετε νά σᾶς δείξω;

I just want to look around.

thélo móno na kitákso
Θέλω μόνο νά κοιτάξω.

I like the one in the window.

moo arési aftó poo éhete stin vitrína
Μοῦ ἀρέσει αὐτό πού ἔχετε στήν βιτρίνα.

Size

What size is this?

ti méyethos íne aftó
Τί μέγεθος εἶναι αὐτό;

I want size . . . .

thélo to méyethos
Θέλω τό μέγεθος . . . .

It is too big/too small.

íne polí meghálo/polí mikró
Εἶναι πολύ μεγάλο/πολύ μικρό.

It is too tight.

íne polí stenó
Εἶναι πολύ στενό.

Have you a larger one?

éhete éna meghalítero
Ἔχετε ἕνα μεγαλύτερο;

Have you a smaller one?

éhete éna mikrótero
Ἔχετε ἕνα μικρότερο;

It is too long.

íne polí makrí
Εἶναι πολύ μακρύ.

It is too short.

íne polí kondó
Εἶναι πολύ κοντό.

It does not fit me.

***th*én moo érhete kalá**
Δέν μοῦ ἔρχεται καλά.

Colour

Have you got it in . . . .

tóhete sto
Τό ἔχετε στό . . .

– beige?

– bez
– μπέζ;

– black?

– mávro
– μαῦρο;

– blue?

– ble
– μπλέ;

– brown?

– kafé
– καφέ;

– cream?	– **krem**
	– *κρέμ;*
– green?	– **prásino**
	– *πράσινο;*
– grey?	– **grízo**
	– *γκρίζο;*
– mauve?	– **mov**
	– *μώβ;*
– orange?	– **portokalí**
	– *πορτοκαλί;*
– pink?	– **roz**
	– *ρόζ;*
– red?	– **kókino**
	– *κόκκινο;*
– white?	– **áspro**
	– *ἄσπρο;*
– yellow?	– **kítrino**
	– *κίτρινο;*
– a lighter colour?	– **se pyó aniktó hróma**
	– *σέ πιό ἀνοικτό χρῶμα;*
– a darker colour?	– **se pyó skoóro hróma**
	– *σέ πιό σκούρο χρῶμα;*
– the same colour?	– **sto íthio hróma**
	– *στό ʼίδιο χρῶμα;*

Some common materials

What's it made of?	**ti ífasma íne**
	Τί ὕφασμα εἶναι;
I'd like it in	**tha to íthela se**
	Θά τό ἤθελα σε . . . .
– chiffon.	– **mooselína**
	– *μουσελίνα.*
– corduroy.	– **veloótho kotle**
	– *βελοῦδο κοτλέ.*
– cotton.	– **vamvakeró (kotón)**
	– *βαμβακερό. (κοτόν)*
– leather.	– **thérma**
	– *δέρμα.*

– linen.

  – **linó**
  – λινό.

– man-made.

  – **sinthetikó**
  – συνθετικό.

– nylon.

  – **'nylon'**
  – νάϋλον.

– rayon.

  – **rayón**
  – ρεγιόν.

– silk.

  – **metaksotó**
  – μεταξωτό.

– suede.

  – **'suede'**
  – σουέντ.

– velvet.

  – **veloótho**
  – βελοῦδο.

– wool

  – **málino**
  – μάλλινο.

I'd like to see materials made in Greece.

  tha íthela na tho elliniká ifásmata
  Θά ἤθελα νά δῶ ἑλληνικά ὑφάσματα.

I'd like something with Greek embroidery.

  tha íthela káti me elinikó kéndima
  Θά ἤθελα κάτι μ' ἑλληνικό κέντημα.

Is it hand-made?

  íne kendiméno me to héri
  Εἶναι κεντημένο μέ τό χέρι;

May I try this?

  boró na to thokimáso
  Μπορῶ νά τό δοκιμάσω;

I'll take it.

  tha to páro
  Θά τό πάρω.

How much is it?

  póso káni
  Πόσο κάνει;

Do you accept credit-cards/ dollars/pounds?

  théheste credit-cards/tholária/ líres
  Δέχεστε κρέντιτ-κάρντς/δολλάρια/ λίρες;

*Please pay the cashier.

  plieróste sto tamío (TAMEION) parakaló
  Πληρῶστε στό ταμεῖο (TAMEION) παρακαλῶ.

May I have a receipt please?

moo *th*ínete mía apó*th*iksi, parakaló
Μοῦ δίνετε μιά ἀπόδειξη, παρακαλῶ;

Complaints

I'd like to change this.

boríte na moo to aláksete aftó, parakaló
Μπορεῖτε νά μοῦ τό ἀλλάξετε αὐτό, παρακαλῶ.

I bought it two days ago/one week ago.

to aghórasa prin apó *th*ío méres/ tin perasméni ev*th*omátha
Τό ἀγόρασα πρίν ἀπό δύο μέρες/τήν περασμένη ἑβδομάδα.

It is dirty/torn.

íne vrómiko/skizméno
Εἶναι βρώμικο/σκισμένο.

It is cracked/broken.

íne raisméno/spazméno
Εἶναι ραϊσμένο/σπασμένο.

It doesn't work.

***th*én *th*oolévi**
Δέν δουλεύει.

I want to see the manager.

thelo na *th*ó ton proistámeno
Θέλω νά δῶ τόν προϊστάμενο.

Shoes

I'd like a pair of shoes.

tha íthela éna zevghári papoótsya
Θά ἤθελα ἕνα ζευγάρι παπούτσια.

I'd like . . . .

tha íthela
Θά ἤθελα . . . .

– shoes.

– papoótsya
– παπούτσια.

– boots.

– bótes
– μπότες.

– sandals.

– pé*th*ila
– πέδιλα.

– tennis shoes.

– papoótsya too ténis
– παπούτσια τοῦ τέννις.

– smart shoes.

– papoótsya ya kalá
– παπούτσια γιά καλά.

– walking shoes.

– papoótsya spor
– παπούτσια σπόρ.

I'm afraid I don't like . . . .

***th*en moo arési**
Δέν μοῦ ἀρέσει . . . .

– the style.

– to shé*th*io
– τό σχέδιο.

– the colour.

– to hróma
– τό χρῶμα.

They are too small/too big.

íne polí mikrá/polí meghála
Εἶναι πολύ μικρά/πολύ μεγάλα.

They are too tight/too wide.

íne polí stená/polí far*th*yá
Εἶναι πολύ στενά/πολύ φαρδειά.

The heels are too high/too low.

ta takoónia íne polí psilá/polí hamilá
Τά τακούνια εἶναι πολύ ψηλά/πολύ χαμηλά.

Do you have the same in . . . .

éhete to íthio se
Ἔχετε τό ἴδιο σέ . . . .

I like them.

moo arésoon
Μοῦ ἀρέσουν.

I don't like them.

***th*en moo arésoon**
Δέν μοῦ ἀρέσουν.

Thank you, good-bye.

ef*h*aristó, hérete
Εὐχαριστῶ, χαίρετε.

CONVERSION TABLES

This is only a general guide, and it is always advisable to try on clothes etc. before buying them.

Women's clothes

	ENGLISH	GREEK		ENGLISH	GREEK
Dresses	32	38	Hats	$6\frac{1}{8}$	50 cm
	34	40		$6\frac{1}{4}$	51
	36	42		$6\frac{3}{8}$	52
	38	44		$6\frac{1}{2}$	53
	40	46		$6\frac{5}{8}$	54
	42	48		$6\frac{3}{4}$	55
				$6\frac{7}{8}$	56
Blouses	30	42		7	57
	32	44		$7\frac{1}{8}$	58
	34	46		$7\frac{1}{4}$	59
	36	48		$7\frac{3}{8}$	60
	38	50		$7\frac{1}{2}$	61
	40	52			
	42	54	Shoes	2	34
				$2\frac{1}{2}$	35
Sweaters	32	42		3	$35\frac{1}{2}$
	34	44		$3\frac{1}{2}$	36
	36	46		4	$36\frac{1}{2}$
	38	48		$4\frac{1}{2}$	$37\frac{1}{2}$
	40	50		5	38
				$5\frac{1}{2}$	$38\frac{1}{2}$
Stockings	8	0		6	$39\frac{1}{4}$
	$8\frac{1}{2}$	1		$6\frac{1}{2}$	40
	9	2		7	$40\frac{1}{2}$
	$9\frac{1}{2}$	3		$7\frac{1}{2}$	41
	10	4		8	42
	$10\frac{1}{2}$	5			
	11	6			

Men's clothes

Hats	ENGLISH	GREEK		Suits & coats	ENGLISH	GREEK
Hats	$6\frac{1}{4}$	51		Suits & coats	36	46
	$6\frac{3}{8}$	52			38	48
	$6\frac{1}{2}$	53			40	50
	$6\frac{5}{8}$	54			42	52
	$6\frac{3}{4}$	55			44	54
	$6\frac{7}{8}$	56			46	56
	7	57				
	$7\frac{1}{8}$	58		Shoes	7	$40\frac{1}{2}$
	$7\frac{1}{4}$	59			8	42
	$7\frac{3}{8}$	60			9	43
	$7\frac{1}{2}$	61			10	44
	$7\frac{5}{8}$	62			11	$45\frac{1}{2}$
	$7\frac{3}{4}$	63			12	47
	$7\frac{7}{8}$	64			13	48
Shirts	13	33		Socks	$9\frac{1}{2}$	39
	$13\frac{1}{2}$	34			10	40
	14	35–36			$10\frac{1}{2}$	41
	$14\frac{1}{2}$	37			11	42
	15	38			$11\frac{1}{2}$	43
	$15\frac{1}{2}$	39			12	44
	$15\frac{3}{4}$	40			$12\frac{1}{2}$	45
	16	41				
	$16\frac{1}{2}$	42				
	17	43				

VOCABULARY

blouse	**i blóoza** 'Η μπλούζα
coat	**to paltó** Τό παλτό
dress	**to foostáni** Τό φουστάνι
jacket (lady's)	**i zakéta** 'Η ζακέτα
jacket (man's)	**to sakáki** Τό σακκάκι
raincoat	**to a*th*iávroho** Τό ἀδιάβροχο
shirts	**ta pookámisa** Τά πουκάμισα
skirt	**i foósta** 'Η φούστα
suit (lady's)	**to tayiér** Τό ταγιέρ
suit (man's)	**to koostóomi** Τό κουστούμι
trousers	**to pandelóni** Τό παντελόμι
underwear	**ta esórooha** Τά ἀ ἐσώρρουχα

I want these clothes . . . .

thélo aftá ta roóha
Θέλω αὐτά τά ροῦχα . . . .

– cleaned.

– na ta katharísete
– νά τά καθαρίσετε.

– pressed only.

– na ta si*th*erósete mónon
– νά τά σιδερώσετε μόνον.

– washed.

– na ta plínete
– νά τά πλύνετε.

Can you . . . .

boríte
Μπορεῖτε . . . .

– get this stain out?

– na katharísete aftón ton leké?
– Νά καθαρίσετε αὐτόν τόν λεκέ;

– mend this invisibly?

– na mandárete, aftó horís na fénete
– νά μαντάρετε αὐτό, χωρίς νά φαίνεται;

– stitch this?	– **na tō rápsete** – *νά τό ράψετε;*
– sew on a button?	– **na válete éna koombí** – *νά βάλετε ἕνα κουμπί;*
– put in a new zip?	– **naláksete to fermooár** – *ν'ἀλλάξετε τό φερμουάρ;*
When will it/they be ready?	**póte tha íne étimo/étima** *Πότε θά εἶναι ἕτοιμο/ἕτοιμα;*
I need it as soon as possible.	**ta thélo óso yínete pyó ghríghora** *Τά θέλω ὅσο γίνεται πιό γρήγορα.*
This isn't mine.	**aftó then íne thikó moo** *Αὐτό δέν εἶναι δικό μου.*
The belt/a button is missing.	**lípi i zóni/éna koombí** *Λείπει ἡ ζώνη/ἕνα κουμπί.*
It is not well cleaned.	**then to éhete katharísi kalá** *Δέν τό ἔχετε καθαρίσει καλά.*
Can you clean it again?	**boríte na to katharísete páli** *Μπορεῖτε νά τό καθαρίσετε πάλι;*

At the Hairdresser or Barber

I'd like to make an appointment for . . . .
tha íthela éna randevoó ya
Θά ἤθελα ἕνα ραντεβοῦ γιά . . . .

I'd like . . . .
thélo . . . .
Θέλω . . . .

– a shampoo and set.
– loósimo ke mizanplí
– λούσιμο καί μίζ-αν-πλί.

– a shampoo only.
– móno loósimo
– μόνο λούσιμο.

– a set with large/small rollers.
– mía mizanplí me meghála/mikrá rolá
– μία μίζ-αν-πλί μέ μεγάλα/μικρά ρολά.

– a blow-dry set.
– mía mizanpli metó pistolaki
– μια μιζ-αν-πλι μέ τό πιστολάκι.

– a cut.
– na moo kópsete ta malyá moo
– νά μοῦ κόψετε τά μαλλιά μου.

– a trim.
– na moo ta kópsete polí lígho
– νά μοῦ τά κόψετε πολύ λίγο.

– a perm.
– mía permanánd
– μία περμανάντ.

– my hair straightened.
– na moo isyósete ta malyá moo
– νά μοῦ ἰσιώσετε τά μαλλιά μου.

– a tint.
– vafí
– βαφή.

– tint with shampoo.
– hromosampooán
– χρωμοσαμπουάν.

– re-styling.
– éna kenoórghio stíl
– ἕνα καινούργιο στύλ.

*How much do you want cut?
póso kondá ta thélete
Πόσο κοντά τά θέλετε;

Not too short.

óhi polí kondá
Ὄχι πολύ κοντά.

Very short.

polí kondá
Πολύ κοντά.

A little more off the . . . .

na ta kópsete lígho akómi
Νά τά κόψετε λίγο ἀκόμη . . . .

– back.

– píso
– πίσω.

– sides.

– sto plái
– στό πλάϊ.

– top.

– epáno
– ἐπάνω.

That is enough, no more.

ftáni, óhi álo
Φτάνει, ὄχι ἄλλο.

*What colour would you like?

ti hróma thélete
Τί χρῶμα θέλετε;

Do you have a colour-chart?

éhete thíghmata vafón
ἔχετε δείγματα βαφῶν;

I want . . . .

thélo
Θέλω . . . .

– the same colour.

– to íthio hróma
– Τό ἴδιο χρῶμα.

– darker.

– pyó skoóro
– πιό σκοῦρο.

– lighter.

– pyó aniktó
– πιό ἀνοικτό.

– roots only.

– tis rízes móno
– τίς ρίζες μόνο.

I want a . . . .

thélo
Θέλω . . . .

– manicure.

– manikioór
– μανικιούρ.

– pedicure.

– pendikoór
– πεντικιούρ.

– leg-wax.

– haláooa
– χαλάουα.

My hair is oily/dry.

ta malyá moo íne lipará/kserá
Τά μαλλιά μου είναι λιπαρά/ξηρά.

The water is cold/hot.

to neró íne krío/polí zestó
Τό νερό είναι κρύο/πολύ ζεστό.

The dryer is too hot/cold.

to sesooár íne polí zestó/krío
Τό σεσουάρ είναι πολύ ζεστό/κρύο.

I'm in a hurry.

viázome
Βιάζομαι.

At the barber's only
I'd like a shave.

ksírisma parakaló
Ξύρισμα παρακαλῶ.

Please cut (a little) my . . . .

parakaló moo kóvete (lígho)
Παρακαλῶ μοῦ κόβετε (λίγο) . . . .

– beard.

– to yéni moo
– τό γένι μου.

– moustache.

– to moostáki moo
– τό μουστάκι μου.

– sideboards.

– tis favorítes moo
– τίς φαβορίτες μου.

Note: Don't forget to tip the hairdresser, barber, and their assistants.

At the Bank

Banks are open: Monday to Friday 8 a.m. to 4 p.m. and Saturday 8 a.m. to 2 p.m.

Can you cash these cheques please?
moo alázete aftá ta chéques parakaló
Μοῦ ἀλλάζετε αὐτά τά τσέκς παρακαλῶ;

Can you change these pounds please?
moo alázete aftés tis líres parakaló
Μοῦ ἀλλάζετε αὐτές τίς λίρες παρακαλῶ;

How much do I get for a pound/dollar?
póso éhi i líra/to tholário
Πόσο ἔχει ἡ λίρα/τό δολλάριο;

Can you give me some small change?
moo thínete meriká psilá parakaló
Μοῦ δίνετε μερικά ψιλά παρακαλῶ;

I think you have made a mistake.
nomízo óti éhete káni éna láthos
Νομίζω ὅτι ἔχετε κάνει ἕνα λάθος.

*Give me your passport please.
to thiavatírio sas, parakaló
Τό διαβατήριο σας, παρακαλῶ.

*Sign here please.
ipoghrápsete ethó, parakaló
Ὑπογράψτε ἐδῶ, παρακαλῶ.

*Go to the cashier.
piyénete sto tamío (tameion)
Πηγαίνετε στό ταμεῖο.

I am expecting some money.
periméno hrímata
Περιμένω χρήματα.

A money order.
mía epitayí
Μία ἐπιταγή.

A cheque from . . . .
éna chéque apó
Ἕνα τσέκ ἀπό . . . .

Has it come?
éhi élthi
ἔχει ἔλθει;

Can you cable my bank?

boríte na tileghrafísete stin trápeza moo
Μπορεῖτε νά τηλεγραφήσετε στην τράπεζα μου;

How long will it take?

se pósi óra tha éhete teliósi
Σέ πόση ὥρα θά ἔχετε τελειώσει;

*Come back . . . .

eláte
Ἐλᾶτε . . . .

– in an hour.

– se mía óra
– σέ μία ὥρα.

– tomorrow morning.

– ávrio to proí
– αὔριο τό πρωί.

– in three days.

– se tris méres
– σέ τρεῖς μέρες.

The Greek currency unit is the drachma. (pronounced **T*h*rahmí**)

(sing.) **i *th*rahmí**   ἡ δραχμή
(plur.) **i *th*rahmés**   οἱ δραχμές
The abrev. used in shops etc., is   δρχ.
1 drachma has 100 leptá   λεπτά

There are coins of 1, 2, 5, 10 and 20 drachmas and bank-notes of 50, 100, 500, and 1000 drachmas.
Also coins of 50 lepta (½ drachma).

Your own table (for inserting the current rate of exchange)

	Drachma	£	£	Drachma
1	drachma			
		1.00		
5	drachmas			
		5.00		
10	drachmas			
		10.00		
50	drachmas			
			0.50p.	
100	drachmas			
			0.10p.	

	Drachma	£	£	Drachma
1000	drachmas			
50	lepta			
			0.1p	

Note: Visitors wishing to change their currencies into Drachmas can apply to any bank in Athens or in the provinces. There are also money changing desks at the entry points to Greece. Several of the offices of the Telecommunications Organization (OTE) and the Post Office (ELTA) will also change foreign currencies. Finally, this can also be done at the reception desks of several hotels and tourist gift shops.

The Post Office, Telephones, Telegrams

Most Post Offices are open Monday to Saturday from 7.30 a.m.–6 p.m. The Central Post Office, 100 Εόλου (*ΑΙΟΛΟΥ*) Street, and the Syntagma Square branch, are also open on Sunday.

Telegrams are *not* taken at Post Offices but at the offices of *OTE* the State Telecommununications Organisation. To send a telegram by phone dial 165 for a telegram abroad and 155 for an internal one.

Telephones Long distance calls are generally made from the *OTE* offices. Telephone call boxes are few in number but you can always make calls from a kiosk or shop. Call boxes accept coins and usually have directions for use, in English.

Stamps are sold at Post Offices. kiosks and hotels.

At the Post Office (*ΕΛΤΑ*)

Post-Office	**tahi*th*romíon**
	ΤΑΧΥΔΡΟΜΕΙΟΝ
Where is the post-office?	**poo íne to tahi*th*romío**
	Ποῦ εἶναι τό ταχυδρομεῖο;

Sending a letter

How much is a letter for England?	**póso káni to ghramatósimo ya tin Anglía**
	Πόσο κάνει τό γραμματόσημο γιά τήν Ἀγγλία;
– by air mail?	**– aeroporikó**
	– ἀεροπορικό;
– by surface mail?	**– apló**
	– ἁπλό;

– express?	– katepíghon
	– κατεπεῖγον;
– registered?	– sistiméno
	– συστημένο;
– recorded delivery?	– me apóthiksi paralavís
	– μέ ἀπόδειξη παραλαβῆς;
I want some stamps please.	thélo meriká ghramatósima parakaló
	Θέλω μερικά γραμματόσημα παρακαλῶ.
I want to send a postal order to	thélo na stílo mía tahithromikí epitayí sto
	Θέλω νά στείλω μία ταχυδρομική ἐπιταγή στό . . . .

Sending a parcel

parcel	to théma Τό δέμα
fragile	éfthrafston Εὔθραυστον
Urgent	epíghon Ἐπεῖγον
I want to send this parcel to	thélo na stílo aftó to théma sto
	Θέλω νά στείλω αὐτό τό δέμα στό . . . .
Do I need to fill in a customs declaration?	prépi na simbliróso thílosi ya to telonío
	Πρέπει νά συμπληρώσω δήλωση γιά τό τελωνεῖο;
How much is it?	póso káni
	Πόσο κάνει;
When will it get there?	póte tha fthási
	Πότε θά φτάσει;

Poste-Restante

Where is the Poste-Restante?	poo íne i póste-Restánte
	Ποῦ εἶναι ἡ πόστ-ρεστάντ;
Is there any post for me?	éhete ghrámata ya ména
	Ἔχετε γράμματα γιά μένα;

*What is your name?	**pos légheste** *Πῶς λέγεστε;*
*Have you got your passport?	**éhete to *th*iavatírio sas** *Ἔχετε τό διαβατήριο σας;*
When is the next delivery?	**póte íne to epómeno tahi*th*romío** *Πότε εἶναι τό ἑπόμενο ταχυδρομεῖο;*
Will you have letters sent on to this address please?	**boríte na stílete ta ghrámata moo safti tin *th*iéfthinsi parakaló** *Μπορεῖτε νά στείλετε τά γράμματα μου σ'αὐτή τήν διεύθυση παρακαλῶ;*

SIGNS IN THE POST OFFICE

ΓΡΑΜΜΑΤΟΣΗΜΑ	stamps
ΔΕΜΑΤΑ	parcels
ΕΠΙΤΑΓΕΣ	money orders

Note: Post-boxes are painted yellow.

OTE *(the State Telecommunications Organisation)*

For telegrams and long-distance calls.

Sending a telegram
(Not taken at the Post Office but at the offices of the Telecommunications Organisation (OTE).

Where is the OTE?	**poo íne o OTÉ** *Ποῦ εἶναι ὁ ΟΤΕ;*
I want to send a telegram to	**thélo na stílo éna tileghráfima sto** *Θέλω νά στείλω ἕνα τηλεγράφημα στό . . . .*
How much is it per word?	**póso káni i léksi** *Πόσο κάνει ἡ λέξη;*

I want to send a telegram with the reply paid.

thélo na stílo éna tilegráfima me pliroméni tin apándisi

Θέλω νά στείλω ἕνα τηλεγράφημα μέ πληρωμένη τήν ἀπάντηση.

How long will it take to get there?

póte tha ftási

Πότε θά φτάση;

Is the night-cable cheaper?

íne to nikterinó, pyó fthinó

Εἶναι τό νυκτερινό πιό φθηνό;

Telephoning

ΕΔΩ ΤΗΛΕΦΩΝΕΙΤΕ   public telephone
ΤΗΛΕΦΩΝΟ ΔΙΑ ΤΟ ΚΟΙΝΟ   public telephone

Is there a phone here?

éhete tiléfono

Ἔχετε τηλέφωνο;

Please may I use the phone?

boró na tilefoníso

Μπορῶ νά τηλεφωνήσω;

Where is the nearest phone please?

poo éhi tiléfono ethó kondá

Ποῦ ἔχει τηλέφωνο ἐδῶ κοντά;

Please could you change this? (money)

parakaló éhete psilá

Παρακαλῶ, ἔχετε ψιλά;

Do you have a telephone directory?

éhete tilefonikó katálogho

Ἔχετε τηλεφωνικό κατάλογο;

Please, can you help me make this call?

parakaló boríte na me voithísete na tilefoníso

Παρακαλῶ, μπορεῖτε νά μέ βοηθήσετε νά τηλεφωνήσω;

Direct dialling
Hello.

embrós

Ἐμπρός.

Do you speak English?

miláte angliká

Μιλᾶτε ἀγγλικά;

This is Tom.

o Tom ethó

Ὁ Τόμ ἐδῶ.

Can I speak to . . .?

boró na milíso ston(M)/stin(F)

Μπορῶ νά μιλήσω στόν/στήν;

*Hold on, please.

periménete parakaló
Περιμένετε παρακαλῶ.

*He/she is not here.

then íne ethó
Δέν εἶναι ἐδῶ.

Tell him/her that Tom phoned.

péste too/tis óti tilefónise o Tom
Πέστε του/της ὅτι τηλεφώνησε ὁ Τόμ.

Thank you, goodbye.

efharistó, hérete
Εὐχαριστῶ, χαίρετε.

Who's speaking?

pyós íne
Ποιός εἶναι;

*You have the wrong number.

éhete láthos arithmó
Ἔχετε λάθος ἀριθμό.

The phone is busy.

milái
μιλάει.

Calls made via the operator

Do you speak English?

miláte angliká
Μιλᾶτε ἀγγλικά;

Is there someone who can speak English?

ipárhi kanís poo na milái angliká
Ὑπάρχει κανείς πού νά μιλάη ἀγγλικά;

I'd like to make a call to England.

thélo na tilefoníso stin Anglía.
Θέλω νά τηλεφωνήσω στήν Ἀγγλία.

The number (in England) is ....

o arithmós (stin Anglía) íne
Ὁ ἀριθμός (στήν Ἀγγλία) εἶναι ....

My number is ....

o thikós moo o arithmós íne
Ὁ δικός μου ὁ ἀριθμός εἶναι ....

*What is your number?

ti arithmó éhete
Τί ἀριθμό ἔχετε;

I'd like to make a personal call to Mr/Mrs

thélo na káno éna prosopikó tilefónima ston kírio/stin kiría
Θέλω νά κάνω ἕνα προσωπικό τηλεφώνημα στόν κύριο/στήν κυρία ....

I'd like to make a reverse charge call.

thélo na hreothí to tilefónima ston paralípti

Θέλω νά χρεωθεῖ τό τηλεφώνημα στόν παραλήπτη.

Can I book a call to England for 8 p.m.?

boró na reserváro éna tilefónima stin Anglía ya tis októ (8) to vráthi

Μπορῶ νά ρεζερβάρω ἕνα τηλεφώνημα στήν 'Αγγλία γιά τίς ὀκτώ (8) τό βράδυ;

How much will it cost for three minutes?

póso tha stihísi ya tría leptá

Πόσο θά στοιχίσει γιά τρία λεπτά;

*The line is engaged.

then éhi ghramí

Δέν ἔχει γραμμή.

*Replace the receiver.

klíste to tiléfono

Κλεῖστε τό τηλέφωνο.

*Hold the line please.

periménete parakaló

Περιμένετε παρακαλῶ.

*There is no answer.

then apandái

Δέν ἀπαντάει.

*The phone is busy.

milái

Μιλάει.

*Try again later.

thokimásete páli arghótera

Δοκιμάσετε πάλι ἀργότερα.

When?

póte

Πότε;

*In three hours.

se tris óres

Σέ τρεῖς ὧρες.

I've been cut off.

mas thiékopsan

Μᾶς διέκοψαν

Please could you reconnect me?

boríte na mas ksanasinthésete parakaló

Μπορεῖτε νά μᾶς ξανασυνδέσετε παρακαλῶ;

This phone is out of order.

aftó to tiléfono íne halasméno

Αὐτό τό τηλέφωνο εἶναι χαλασμένο.

Medical Treatment

Note: To call an ambulance dial 166.

Where is	**poo íne** *Πο̃υ εἶναι . . . .*
– a doctor?	**– énas yiatrós** *– ἕνας γιατρός;*
– his surgery?	**– to iatrío** *– τό ἰατρεῖο;*
– the hospital?	**– to nosokomío** *– τό νοσοκομεῖο;*
Call an ambulance.	**tilefonìste na élthi tón próton voithión** *Τηλεφωνῆστε νά ἔλθει τῶν πρώτων βοηθειῶν.*

PARTS OF THE BODY

abdomen	**i kilyá**	*ἡ κοιλιά*
ankle	**o astrághalos**	*ὁ ἀστράγαλος*
arm	**to héri**	*τό χέρι*
back	**i pláti**	*ἡ πλάτη*
bladder	**i kístis**	*ἡ κύστις*
blood	**to éma**	*τό αἷμα*
bone	**to kókalo**	*τό κόκκαλο*
bowels	**ta éndera**	*τά ἔντερα*
chest	**to stíthos**	*τό στῆθος*
ear	**to aftí** (pl) **aftyá**	*τό αὐτί (αὐτιά)*
elbow	**o angónas**	*ὁ ἀγκώνας*
eye	**to máti** (pl) **mátya**	*τό μάτι (μάτια)*
face	**to prósopo**	*τό πρόσωπο*
finger	**to tháktilo**	*τό δάκτυλο*

foot	**to póthi** *τό πόδι*
gland	**o athénas** *ὀ ἀδένας*
hair	**ta malyá** *τά μαλλιά*
hand	**to héri** *τό χέρι*
head	**to kefáli** *τό κεφάλι*
heart	**i karthyá** *ἡ καρδιά*
joint	**i árthrosi** *ἡ ἄρθρωση*
kidney	**to nefró** *τό νεφρό*
knee	**to ghónato** *τό γόνατο*
leg	**to póthi** *τό πόδι*
lip	**to híli (pl) hílya** *τό χεῖλι (τά χείλια)*
liver	**to sikóti** *τό συκώτι*
lung	**o pnévmonas** *ὀ πνεύμονας*
mouth	**to stóma** *τό στόμα*
muscle	**o mís** *ὀ μῦς*
neck	**o lemós** *ὀ λαιμός*
nerve	**tó névro** *τό νεῦρο*
nervous system	**to nevrikó sístima** *τό νευρικό σύστημα*
nose	**i míti** *ἡ μύτη*
rib	**to plevró** *τό πλευρό*
shoulder	**o ómos** *ὀ ὦμος*
skin	**to thérma** *τό δέρμα*
spine	**i sponthilikí stíli** *ἡ σπονδυλική στήλη*
stomach	**to stomáhi** *τό στομάχι*
throat	**o lemós** *ὀ λαιμός*
toe	**to tháktilo pothyoó** *τό δάκτυλο ποδιοῦ*
tongue	**i ghlósa** *ἡ γλῶσσα*
tonsils	**i amighthalés** *οἱ ἀμυγδαλές*
tooth	**to thóndi** *τό δόντι*
urine	**tá oóra** *τά οὖρα*
vein	**í fléva** *ἡ φλέβα*
wrist	**o karpós** *ὀ καρπός*

At the doctor's

Please call a doctor (at once).	**parakaló fonákste éna yiatró (amésos)** *Παρακαλῶ φωνᾶξτε ἕνα γιατρό (ἀμέσως).*
I must see a doctor.	**prépi na tho éna yiatró** *Πρέπει νά δῶ ἕνα γιατρό.*
Must I make an appointment?	**prépi na klíso randevoó** *Πρέπει νά κλείσω ραντεβοῦ;*
Does he speak English?	**milái Angliká** *Μιλάει ἀγγλικά;*
Can you recommend one that does?	**boríte na moo sistísete éna yiatró poo na milái angliká** *Μπορεῖτε νά μοῦ συστήσετε ἕνα γιατρό πού νά μιλάει ἀγγλικά;*

Most frequent complaints

My stomach *aches* (see parts of of body).	**me ponái to stomáhi moo** *Μέ πονάει τό στομάχι μου.*
I have a *pain* here.	**ého énan póno ethó** *Ἔχω ἕναν πόνο ἐδῶ.*
I feel	**ého** *Ἔχω ....*
– depressed.	**– katáthlipsi** *– κατάθλιψη.*
– dizzy.	**– záles** *– ζάλες.*
– faint.	**– lipothimía** *– λιποθυμία.*
– nauseous.	**– tási ya emetó** *– τάση γιά ἐμετό.*
– shivery.	**– ríyi** *– ρίγη.*
I've got	**ého** *Ἔχω ....*

– a cold.
– **kriósi**
– κρυώσει.

– constipation.
– **thiskiliótita**
– δυσκοιλιότητα.

– a cough.
– **víha**
– βήχα.

– cramp.
– **krámba**
– κράμπα.

– diarrhoea.
– **thiária**
– διάρροια.

– haemorrhage.
– **emorayía**
– αἱμορραγία.

– haemorrhoids.
– **emoroíthes**
– αἱμορροΐδες.

– indigestion.
– **thispepsía**
– δυσπεψία.

– migraine.
– **imikranía**
– ἡμικρανία.

– pains all over.
– **pónoos pandoó**
– πόνους παντοῦ.

– period pains.
– **pónoos perióthoo**
– πόνους περιόδου.

– rash.
– **eksánthima**
– ἐξάνθημα.

– sore throat.
– **ponólemo**
– πονόλαιμο.

– stiff neck.
– **pyástike o lemós moo**
– πιάστηκε ὁ λαιμός μου.

– sunburn.
– **éngavma ilíoo**
– ἔγκαυμα ἡλίου.

– sunstroke.
– **ilíasi**
– ἡλίαση.

– a temperature.
– **piretó**
– πυρετό.

– tonsilitis.
– **amighthalítitha**
– ἀμυγδαλίτιδα.

I've been stung by a bee (wasp).
me tsímbise mélisa (sfíka)
Μέ τσίμπησε μέλισσα/σφῆκα.

I have stepped on a sea-urchin.
pátisa ahinó
Πάτησα ἀχινό.

I've been stung by a jelly-fish.
íne apó tsoóhtra
Εἶναι ἀπό τσούχτρα

I have been bitten by a dog/snake.
me *th*ángase skílos/fí*th*i
Μέ δάγκασε σκῦλος/φίδι.

I've burned/cut/twisted (my hand). (see parts of body)
ékapsa/ékopsa/stramboóliksa (to héri moo)
Ἔκαψα/ἔκοψα/στραμπούληξα. (τά χέρι μου)

My nose won't stop bleeding.
i míti moo tréhi éma sinéhia
Ἡ μύτη μου τρέχει αἷμα συνέχεια.

I've been vomiting.
ékana emetó
Ἔκανα ἐμετό.

I keep vomiting.
káno sinéhia emetó
Κάνω συνέχεια ἐμετό.

I have no appetite.
***th*en ého óreksi**
Δέν ἔχω ὄρεξη.

I can't . . . .
***th*en boró na**
Δέν μπορῶ νά . . . .

– breathe.
– anapnéfso
– ἀναπνεύσω.

– eat anything.
– fáo típota
– φάω τίποτα.

– pass water.
– ooríso
– οὐρήσω.

– sleep.
– kimithó
– κοιμηθῶ.

I think I've got . . . .
nomízo óti ého
Νομίζω ὅτι ἔχω . . . .

– flu.
– ghrípi
– γρίππη.

– food poisoning
– *th*ilitiríasi apó trófima
– δηλητηρίαση ἀπό τρόφιμα.

– tonsilitis.	**– amigh*th*alít*th*a** – ἀμυγδαλίτιδα.
– sinusitis.	**– ighmorítit*h*a** – ἰγμορίτιδα.
– sunstroke.	**– ilíasi** – ἡλίαση.
– urinary infection.	**– oorolímoksi** – οὐρολοίμωξη.

Doctor's questions

*Where does it hurt?	**poo sas poní** *Ποῦ σᾶς πονεῖ;*
*How long have you had this pain?	**póso keró éhete aftón ton póno** *Πόσο καιρό ἔχετε αὐτόν τόν πόνο;*
*Does that hurt you?	**sas poní e*th*ó** *Σᾶς πονεῖ ἐδῶ;*
*A lot or a little?	**polí i lígho** *Πολύ ἤ λίγο;*
*Is this the first time you've had this?	**íne i próti forá poo to pathénete aftó** *Εἶναι ἡ πρώτη φορά πού τό παθαίνετε αὐτό;*
*How long has it been like this?	**póso keró esthánesthe étsi** *Πόσο καιρό αἰσθάνεσθε ἔτσι;*
*Are you allergic to any medicines?	**se ti fármaka ísthe alerghikós** *Σέ τί φάρμακα εἶσθε ἀλλεργικός;*

Personal details and requests

Can I have a prescription for . . .?	**boríte na moo *th*ósete mía sintayí ya** *Μπορεῖτε νά μοῦ δώσετε μιά συνταγή γιά . . .;*
Can you inoculate me against . . .?	**boríte na moo kánete émvólio ya** *Μπορεῖτε νά μοῦ κάνετε ἐμβόλιο γιά . . .;*

I am on the pill.	**pérno to andisiliptikó hápi** Παίρνω τό ἀντισυλληπτικό χάπι.
I take medicine for	**pérno fármako ya** Παίρνω φάρμακο γιά ....
I've lost my	**éhasa ....** Ἔχασα ....
– pills.	**– ta hápya moo** – τά χάπια μου.
– tranquillisers.	**– ta iremistiká hápya moo** – τά ἠρεμιστικά χάπια μου.
– prescription.	**– tin sintayí moo** – τήν συνταγή μου.
– my medicine.	**– to farmakó moo** – τό φάρμακό μου.
– my glasses.	**– ta yialiá moo** – τά γυαλιά μου.
I'm allergic to	**ého aleryía sto/stin** Ἔχω ἀλλεργία στό/στήν ....
I'm asthmatic.	**ipoféro apó ásthma** Ὑποφέρω ἀπό ἄσθμα.
I'm a diabetic.	**íme *thiavitikós*** Εἶμαι διαβητικός.
I'm epileptic.	**íme epiliptikós** Εἶμαι ἐπιληπτικός.
I had a heart attack.	**íha mia kar*th*iakí prosvolí** Εἶχα μιά καρδιακή προσβολή.
I have a heart condition.	**ipoféro apó tin kar*th*yá moo** Ὑποφέρω ἀπό τήν καρδιά μου.
I'm pregnant.	**periméno moró** Περιμένω μωρό.
I'm worried about my baby.	**anisihó polí ya to moró moo** Ἀνησυχῶ πολύ γιά τό μωρό μου.
He won't eat/sleep.	***then* trói/*then* kimáte** Δέν τρώει/δέν κοιμᾶται.
He can't swallow.	***then* borí na katapyí** Δέν μπορεῖ νά καταπιεῖ.

How much do I owe you?	**ti sas ofílo** *Τί σᾶς ὀφείλω;*

Περαστικά (**perastiká**) means 'Get well' and is the usual thing to say to someone who feels ill.

At the dentist

dentist	**o*th*ondoyiatrós** *ὀδοντογιατρός*
My tooth hurts (very badly).	**to *th*óndi moo ponái (pára polí)** *τό δόντι μου πονάει (πάρα πολύ).*
A filling has come out.	**moo éfiye éna voóloma** *Μοῦ ἔφυγε ἕνα βούλωμα.*
A filling has broken.	**éna voóloma éspase** *Ἕνα βούλωμα ἔσπασε.*
My tooth has broken.	**to *th*óndi moo éspase** *Τό δόντι μου ἔσπασε.*
I don't want it extracted.	***th*en thélo na to vghálete** *Δέν θέλω νά τό βγάλετε.*
Can you fill it?	**boríte na to voolósete** *Μπορεῖτε νά τόυ βουλώσετε;*
My gums are sore/bleeding.	**ta oóla moo íne erethisména/ matónoon** *Τά οὐλα μου εἶναι ἐρεθισμένα ματώνουν.*
I've broken my denture.	**éspasa tin o*th*ondostihía moo** *Ἔσπασα τήν ὀδοντοστοιχία μου.*
Can you repair it?	**boríte na tin *th*iorthósete** *Μπορεῖτε νά τήν διορθώσετε;*
When should I come again?	**póte na ksanártho** *Πότε νά ξανάρθω;*
How much do I owe you?	**ti sas ofílo** *Τί σᾶς ὀφείλω;*
Can I make an appointment for . . .?	**boró ná klíso éna randevoó ya** *Μπορῶ νά κλείσω ἕνα ραντεβοῦ γιά . . .;*
As soon as possible.	**óso yínete pyo ghríghora** *Ὅσο γίνεται πιό γρήγορα.*

Entertainment

General

I would like to go to . . . .　**tha íthela na páo**
Θά ἤθελα νά πάω . . . .

– a ball.　**– séna horó**
– σ'ἕνα χορό.

– the ballet.　**– sto baléto**
– στό μπαλλέτο.

– the casino.　**– séna cazíno**
– σ'ἕνα καζίνο.

– a classical Greek tragedy.　**– se mía arhéa elinikí**
　　　traghot*h*ía
– σέ μιά ἀρχαία ἑλληνική τραγωδία.

– the cinema.　**– sto sinemá (ston kinimatoghráfo)**
–στό σινεμά (στόν κινηματογράφο).

– the circus.　**– séna tsírko**
– σ'ἕνα τσίρκο.

– a concert.　**– se mía sinavlía (séna concérto)**
– σέ μιά συναυλία. (σ'ἕνα
　　κονσέρτο)

– a discotheque.　**– séna 'discothéque'**
– σ'ἕνα ντισκοτέκ.

– a fair.　**– séna paniyíri**
– σ'ἕνα πανηγῦρι.

– the wine festival.　**– sto festivál too krasyoó**
– στό φεστιβάλ τοῦ κρασιοῦ.

– a film.　**– séna 'film'**
– σ'ἕνα φίλμ.

– see folk dancing.　**– na *th*o laikoós horoós**
– νά δῶ λαϊκούς χορούς.

– a jazz-club.	– **n'akoóso jazz** – *ν'ἀκούσω τζάζ.*
– a night club.	– **séna 'night club' (nihterinó kéndro)** – *σ'ἕνα νάϊτ-κλάμπ. (νυχτερινό κέντρο)*
– the opera.	– **stin ópera** – *στήν ὄπερα.*
– a theatre.	– **sto théatro** – *στό θέατρο.*
– the zoo.	– **ston zooloyikó kípo** – *στόν ζωολογικό κῆπο.*

In the summer, ancient drama is presented at the open theatre of Herodus Atticus (near the Acropolis) or at Epidauros (in the Peloponnese) by the National Greek Theatre Company. These theatres are also used for orchestral concerts, opera and ballet performances by companies from abroad. Try and go to a concert by moonlight – it is very romantic! At the open-air theatre on the hill of Philopappou in Athens, you can see the Greek national (folk) dances performed. For advance information about the artistic events during the summer festival, about 'Sound and Light' performances, wine festivals etc. inquire at all NTOG offices abroad or in Greece.

Cinema/Theatre

In the summer most cinemas and theatres are in the open air. Performances start when it gets dark. Tickets are more expensive downstairs (**platía**); cheaper upstairs (**eksóstis**). Foreign films are shown in the original language with Greek sub-titles.

At both theatres and cinemas you tip the usherette after she has shown you to your seat.

What is on?	**ti pézi** *Τί παίζει;*

Is it a . . . .
íne
Εἶναι . . . .

– comedy?
– como*th*ía
– κωμωδία;

– drama?
– *th*ráma
– δρᾶμα;

– musical?
– 'musical'
– μιούζικαλ;

– revue?
– epitheórisi
– ἐπιθεώρηση;

– thriller?
– astinomikó
– ἀστυνομικό;

– western?
– 'western'
– γουέστερν;

– Greek film?
– elinikó film
– ἑλληνικό φίλμ;

– English/American film.
– anglikó/amerikániko film
– ἀγγλικό/ἀμερικάνικο φίλμ

Ticket(s)
isitírio (isitíria)
Εἰσιτήριο (εἰσιτήρια)

Two tickets please . . . .
th*í*o isitíria parakaló**
Δύο εἰσιτήρια παρακαλῶ . . . .

– in the stalls.
– stin platía
– στήν πλατεία.

– in the balcony.
– ston eksósti
– στόν ἐξώστη.

– in the box (theatre).
– sto theorío
– στό θεωρεῖο.

at the . . . .
– back.
– píso
– πίσω.

– front.
– embrós
– ἐμπρός.

– middle.
– sti mési
– στή μέση.

– side.
– sto plái
– στό πλάϊ.

For . . . .
ya
Γιά . . . .

– the evening performance.
– tin vrathiní
– τήν βραδυνή.

– the matinée.
– tin apoyevmatiní
– τήν ἀπογευματινή.

– today.
– símera
– σήμερα.

– tomorrow.
– ávrio
– αὔριο.

– next week.
– tin áli evthomátha
– τήν άλλη ἐβδομάδα.

What time does it start/end?
ti óra arhízi/telióni
Τί ὤρα ἀρχίζει/τελειώνει;

May I have a programme?
éna próghrama parakaló
Ἔνα πρόγραμμα παρακαλῶ;

ΑΚΑΤΑΛΛΗΛΟΝ (akatálilon)
Certificate A – Children under 18 are not admitted.

No children under age are admitted.
Certificate A 13 – Children under 13 are not admitted.

Indoor games

Would you like to play . . . .
thélete na péksoome
Θέλετε νά παίξουμε . . . .

– backgammon?
– távli
– τάβλι;

– billiards?
– bilyártho
– μπιλλιάρδο;

– bridge?
– 'bridge'
– μπρίτζ;

– cards?
– hartyá
– χαρτιά;

– chess?
– skáki
– σκάκι;

– table-tennis?
– ping-pong
– πίνγκ-πόνγκ·

Cards	**ta hartyá**
	Τά χαρτιά
clubs	**ta spathyá**
	τά σπαθιά
diamonds	**ta kará**
	τά καρρά
hearts	**i koópes**
	οί κοῦπες
spades	**i píkes**
	οί πίκες
ace	**o ásos**
	ὁ ἄσσος
king	**o ríghas**
	ὁ ρήγας
queen	**i dáma**
	ἡ ντάμα
jack	**o valés**
	ὁ βαλές
dice	**ta zárya**
	τά ζάρια

Note: If you would like to play chemin-de-fer, roulette, baccarat, Black Jack or dice, Mont Parnes, the *Casino* on top of Parnitha Mountain, will be the place to visit. There are other casinos, in Rhodes and Corfu.

Sports: outdoor games

Matches

I would like to go to a . . .	**tha íthela na páo séna**
	Θά ἤθελα νά πάω σ'ἕνα . . . .
– basket-ball match.	**– 'basket-ball match'**
	– μπάσκετ-μπώλ μάτς.
– boxing match.	**– aghóna box (pyghmahias)**
	– ἀγώνα μπόξ (πυγμαχιας)
– football match.	**– 'football match'**
	– φούτ-μπώλ μάτς.

– wrestling match
– **aghóna pális**
– ἀγῶνα πάλης.

Football

Where is the football stadium?
poo íne to státhio (yípetho) too 'football'
Ποῦ εἶναι τό στάδιο (γήπεδο) τοῦ φούτ-μπώλ

Are there any seats?
éhi thésis
Ἔχει θέσεις;

How much are they?
póso kánoon
Πόσο κάνουν;

Are the seats in the sun or shade?
íne aftés i thésis ston ílio i stín skiá
Εἶναι αὐτές οἱ θέσεις στόν ἥλιο ἤ στήν σκιά;

I would like seats in the shade.
thélo thésis stin skiá
Θέλω δέσεις στήν σκιά.

What day is the football match on?
pyá méra éhi match football
Ποιά μέρα ἔχει μάτς φούτ-μπώλ;

What time does it start?
ti óra arhízi
τι ὥρα ἀρχίζει;

Horse races

Horse Races
ipothromíes
Ἱπποδρομίες

Where is the race course?
poo íne o ipóthromos
Ποῦ εἶναι ὁ ἱππόδρομος;

Which is the favourite?
pyó íne to favorí
Ποιό εἶναι τό φαβορί;

50 drachmas to win on . . . .
penínda *thrahmés* ganyán sto
Πενήντα δραχμές γκανιάν στό . . . .

50 dr. a place on . . . .
penínda *thrahmés* plasé sto
Πενήντα δραχμές πλασέ στό . . . .

50 dr. each way on . . . .
50 *thrahmés* síntheto sto
Πενήντα δραχμές σύνθετο στό . . . .

Participating

I would like to . . . .
– go fishing.

– go game-shooting.

– play golf.

– go to a gymnasium.

– go to a swimming pool.

– play tennis.

– do water-skiing.

Can I hire . . . .

– golf clubs?

– tennis rackets?

tha íthela
Θά ἤθελα . . . .
– na pá oya psánema
– νά πάω γιά ψάρεμα.
– na páo ya kiníyi
– νά πάω γιά κυνῆγι.
– na pékso 'golf'
– νά παίξω γκόλφ.
– na páo séna yimnastírio
– νά πάω σ᾽ ἕνα γυμναστήριο.
– na kolimbíso se pisína
– νά κολυμπήσω σέ πισίνα.
– na pékso 'tennis'
– νά παίξω τέννις.
– na káno thalásio ski
– νά κάνω θαλάσσιο σκί.
boró na nikyáso
Μπορῶ νά νοικιάσω . . . .
– bastoónia too golf
– μπαστούνια τοῦ γκόλφ;
– rakétes too 'tennis'
– ρακέτες τοῦ τέννις;

The Beach

Where is a sandy beach near here?
poo éhi amoothyá ethó kondá
Ποῦ ἔχει ἀμμουδιά ἐδῶ κοντά;

Where is a beach with pebbles?
poo éhi plaz me halíki;
Ποῦ ἔχει πλάζ μέ χαλίκι;

Is the sea clean?
íne katharí i thálasa
Εἶναι καθαρή ἡ θάλασσα;

Is it deep here?
íne vathiá ethó
Εἶναι βαθειά ἐδῶ;

Is there a strong current here?
éhi thinató révma ethó
Ἔχει δυνατό ρεῦμα ἐδῶ;

Is there any shade on the beach?
éhi kathóloo skiá stin plaz
Ἔχει καθόλου σκιά στήν πλάζ;

Are there any cabins/showers/a tap?
éhi cambínes/doós/vrísi
ἔχει καμπίνες/ντούς/βρύση;

The sea is dirty here.
i thálasa íne vrómiki ethó
Ἡ θάλασσα εἶναι βρώμικη ἐδῶ.

The sea is too deep here.
i thálasa íne polí vathyá ethó
Ἡ θάλασσα εἶναι πολύ βαθειά ἐδῶ.

It is rocky.
éhi vráhia
Ἔχει βράχια

It has jelly-fish/sea-urchins.
éhi tsoóhtres/ahinoós
Ἔχει τσούχτρες/ἀχινούς.

It is dangerous.
íne epikínthini
Εἶναι ἐπικύνδινη.

Where is the best place for . . . .
pyó íni to kalítero méros ya
Ποιό εἶναι τό καλύτερο μέρος γιά . . .

– fishing?
– psárema
– φάρεμα;

– under-water fishing?
– ipovríhio psárema
– ὑποβρύχιο ψάρεμα;

– water-skiing?
– thalasió ski
– θαλασσιό σκί;

– surfing?

– '**surf**'

– σέρφ;

Hiring

I would like to hire . . . .

tha íthela na nikyáso

Θά ἤθελα νά νοικιάσω . . . .

– a deck-chair.

– **mía polithróna (chaise-longue)**

– μιά πολυθρόνα (σεζλόγκ).

– a sun shade.

– **mía (úmbrélla) ya ton ílio**

– μία ὀμπρέλλα γιά τόν ἤλιο.

– flippers.

– **vatrahopéthila**

– βατραχοπέδιλα.

– a skin-diving outfit.

– **mia stolí ya ipovríhio psárema**

– μια στολή γιά ὑποβρύχιο ψάρεμα.

– water-skis.

– **thalásia ski**

– θαλάσσια σκί.

– a canoe.

– **éna kanó**

– ἕνα κανώ.

– a rowing boat.

– **mía várka**

– μιά βάρκα.

– a motor boat.

– **mía várka me mihaní**

– μιά βάρκα μέ μηχανή.

– a sailing boat.

– **mía várka me paní**

– μιά βάρκα μέ πανί.

How much is it for . . . .

póso káni ya

Πόσο κάνει γιά . . . .

– an hour?

– **mía óra**

– μιά ὥρα;

– all morning?

– **ya ólo to proí**

– γιά ὅλο τό πρωΐ;

– all day?

– **ya óli tin iméra**

– γιά ὅλη τήν ἡμέρα;

Note: Bathing is very enjoyable in wonderfully clear water, and safe, for there are no tides or sharks. But beware of sea-urchins and jellyfish! If you do step on a sea-urchin try and soften the affected area with oil before attempting to remove the spikes (this is what the locals do).

Sightseeing

Where is the Tourist Office?

poo íne to ghrafía Toorismoó
Ποῦ εἶναι τό γραφεῖο τομρισμοῦ;

What hours is it open?

ti óres íne aniktó
Τί ὥρες εἶναι ἀνοικτό;

Where is the Tourist Police?

poo íne i Tooristikí astinomía
*Ποῦ εἶναι ἡ τουριστική
'Αστυνομία;*

Is there an office that organises
excursions?

**éhi grafío poo orghanóni
ekthromés ethó**
*Ἔχει γραφεῖο πού ὀργανώνει
ἐκδρομές ἐδῶ;*

How much is this excursion?

póso kostízi aftí i ekthromí
Πόσο κοστίζει αὐτή ἡ ἐκδρομή;

What time does it start/end?

**ti óra tha ksekinísoome/tha
yirísoome**
*Τί ὥρα θά ξεκινήσουμε/θά
γυρίσουμε;*

We would like a guide who speaks
English.

**thélome éna ksenaghó poo na
milái anglíká**
*θέλομε ἔνα ξεναγό πού νά μιλάει
ἀγγλικά.*

We don't need a guide.

then mas hriázete ksenaghós
Δέν μᾶς χρειάζεται ξεναγός.

How much should we pay the
guide?

póso pérni o ksenaghós
Πόσο παίρνει ὁ ξεναγός;

Is there somebody to show us the
way?

**ipárhi kanís na mas thíksi ton
thrómo**
*'Υπάρχει κανείς νά μᾶς δείξει τόν
δρόμο;*

Where can I get a map of . . .?	**poo boró naghoráso éna hárti tis** *Ποῦ μπορῶ νά ἀγοράσω ἕνα χάρτη* *τῆς . . .;*
Have you got a guide-book for . . .?	**éhete éna tooristikó othighó ya** *Ἔχετε ἕνα τουριστικό ὁδηγό* *γιά . . .;*
In English?	**sta angliká** *Στ' ἀγγλικά;*
What do you recommend me to visit?	**pyá méri tha me symvoolévate na** **episkefthó** *Ποιά μέρη θά μέ συμβουλεύατε νά* *ἐπισκεφθῶ;*
Where is it?	**poo íne** *Ποῦ εἶναι;*
Which is the most interesting. . . .	**pyó íne to pyó enthiaféron** *Ποιό εἶναι τό πιό ἐνδιαφέρον . . . .*
– museum?	**– moosío** *– μουσεῖο;*
– monastery?	**– monastíri** *– μοναστήρι;*
– cemetery?	**– nekrotafío** *– νεκροταφεῖο;*
– archaeological site?	**– arheoloyikós tópos** *– ἀρχαιολογικός τόπος;*
Where is/are	**poó íne** *Ποῦ εἶναι . . . .*
– the antiquities?	**– i arheótites** *– οἱ ἀρχαιότητες;*
– the art gallery?	**– i pinakothíki** *– ἡ πινακοθήκη;*
– the castle?	**– to kástro** *– τό κάστρο;*
– the catacombs?	**– i katakómves** *– οἱ κατακόμβες;*
– the cathedral?	**– i mitrópoli** *– ἡ μητρόπολη;*

– the cave?	– **to spíleo**
	– *τό σπήλαιο;*
– the cemetery?	– **to nekrotafío**
	– *τό νεκροταφεῖο;*
– the church?	– **i eklisía**
	– *ἡ ἐκκλησία;*
– the fortress?	– **to froório**
	– *τό φρούριο;*
– the fountain?	– **i piyí**
	– *ἡ πηγή;*
– the market?	– **i aghorá**
	– *ἡ ἀγορά;*
– the monastery?	– **to monastíri**
	– *τό μοναστῆρι;*
– the museum?	– **to moosío**
	– *τό μουσεῖο;*
– the old part of the town?	– **i palyá pólis**
	– *ἡ παλια πόλης;*
– the palace?	– **to paláti**
	– *τό παλάτι;*
– the stadium?	– **to státhio**
	– *τό στάδιο;*
– the statue?	– **to ághalma**
	– *τό ἄγαλμα;*
– the temple (ancient)?	– **o naós (arhéos)**
	– *ὁ ναός (ἀρχαῖος);*
– the tomb?	– **o táfos**
	– *ὁ τάφος;*
When is the museum open?	**póte íne to moosío aniktó**
	Πότε εἶναι τό μουσεῖο ἀνοικτό;
How much does it cost to go in?	**póso éhi i ísothos**
	Πόσο ἔχει ἡ εἴσοδος;
Are there any days when admission is free?	**pyés méres íne i ísothos elefthéra**
	Ποιές μέρες εἶναι ἡ εἴσοδος ἐλευθέρα;

Is there a reduction for students/ children?

éhi ékptosi ya toos fitités/ ta pethyá
Έχει ἔκπτωση γιά τούς φοιτητές/ τά παιδιά;

Can I take pictures?

boró na páro fotoghrafíes
Μπορῶ νά πάρω φωτογραφίες;

Architecture
Doric order
Ionic order
Corinthian order

thorikós rithmós *Δωρικός ρυθμός*
ionikós rithmós *Ἰωνικός ρυθμός*
korinthiakós rithmós
   Κορινθιακός ρυθμός

NOTICES

ΑΠΑΓΟΡΕΥΟΝΤΑΙ ΑΙ
   ΦΩΤΟΓΡΑΦΙΚΑΙ ΜΗΧΑΝΑΙ

No cameras allowed

ΑΠΑΓΟΡΕΥΟΝΤΑΙ ΟΙ
   ΦΩΤΟΓΡΑΦΙΕΣ

Photographs are prohibited

ΕΙΣΟΔΟΣ ΕΛΕΥΘΕΡΑ

Admission Free

ΜΗΝ ΕΓΓΙΖΕΤΕ

DO NOT TOUCH

Note: Museums are generally open from 8 a.m. to 1 p.m. and 3 p.m. to 6 p.m. in summer, 9 a.m. to 3.30 p.m. in winter, but with local variations. Often closed on Mondays or Tuesdays. *Free admission* is on Sundays. *Students* (possessing student's card) pay a special low entrance fee.

A list of the Museums and Art Galleries, describing their collections and giving information about days and hours of admission, can be obtained from the NTOG.

Food and Drink

The Greek kitchen offers many exciting dishes which are even more enjoyable when eaten under aromatic pine trees, next to the sparkling Aegean.

A tentacle of octopus baked on charcoal and washed down with a glass of retsina, is quite a different experience in the local tavernas so temptingly scattered along the beaches, than under northern grey skies or inside a luxury hotel. Try and eat where the Greeks eat – in a **tavérna**. They are found everywhere but the cooking varies widely from place to place as it is usually done by the owner and his wife.

If you are puzzled by the menu go to the kitchen and choose what you want. Some dishes, usually the fish, are sold by the kilo (2.2 lb). Make your choice and he will weigh them and then cook them in the way you wish (fried or grilled is best) while you sit at your table, nibbling away at the **mezethákia** (appetisers) and drinking wine.

The more obscure tavernas, hidden away in the side-streets, are likely to be more intimate, better in atmosphere and priced more cheaply.

In Athens there are many tavernas in the oldest part of the city (**Plaka**, Πλάκα) at the foot of the Acropolis but unfortunately many have become chi-chi and garish. If you want sea food it is worth visiting the coastal suburbs which are readily accessible from the centre by bus or underground.

Prices at tavernas and restaurants vary a lot. Although your bill will include the service charge (which is the waiter's tip) it is customary to leave an extra 5–10% for the waiter. You should also remember 'the mikrós', the young boy who helps the waiter and who, unless tipped, gets nothing at all. For him the tip should be left on the table (and not on the plate on which the bill is presented).

Meal times: Greeks eat relatively late. Lunch is from one to three o'clock and dinner from eight until midnight or later.

Almost everything is shut during the afternoon, siesta time, and starts up again around 4 p.m.

Other places where you can eat and drink:

1. **Ghalaktopolíon** (*ΓΑΛΑΚΤΟΠΩΛΕΙΟΝ*), a dairy where you can order yogurt, a bowl of rice pudding or something sweet such as baclavas. Also milk and delicious honey, can be bought there.

2. **Zacharoplastíó** (*ΖΑΧΑΡΟΠΛΑΣΤΕΙΟΝ*), a pastry shop where you can order ouzo, ice-cream, coffee, pastries, light snacks, and cakes.

3. **Kafenío** (*ΚΑΦΕΝΕΙΟΝ*), is a coffee house. This represents a way of Greek living. From the luxurious to the very modest (maybe only three chairs and a table). You sit as long as you like to sip coffee, watch the people go by, contemplate life, wait for your friends, argue politics, play **távli** (backgammon) – a place to rest and gaze and forget sorrow. Greek coffee is the same as Turkish coffee. It is served in a small cup and it is made of fine-ground coffee boiled with water and sugar (if desired) in a special pot called '**bríki**'. There are some thirty-six ways of making it but the following ones are the most usual ways of ordering:

> (a) **skétos** (no sugar)
> (b) **métrios** (medium sweet)
> (c) **varís ghlikos** (strong and sweet)

If you like, you can have your fortune told from your cup of coffee (drink it, turn the cup upside down, let the coffee grains settle and there, in the thick black mess, lies your future . . .).

If you don't want Greek coffee, the most usual alternative is **Nescafé** which is the word used for all instant coffee. In larger towns, in hotels and in more modern establishments you can have espresso or any other variety of coffee.

There are numerous places for a fast snack on the premises, or to take away. A typically Greek snack is **souvláki** (kebab), **tirópita** (cheese-pie), **piróski** (made with frankfurters or minced meat), **spanakópita** (spinach pie) and **kreatópita** (meat pie). There are many of these shops selling this kind of food for very reasonable prices. They also sell sandwiches, pizzas and other sweet pies such as **boughátsa** (with semolina filling) or **milopíta** (apple pie).

In fact it is never a problem to find somewhere to eat in Greece.

Note: If you visit remote areas or the smaller islands it would be a good idea to take your own coffee and tea.

Drinks

Beer (**bíra** – *ΜΠΥΡΑ*)
Greek beer (FIX-*ΦΙΧ*, ALFA-*ΑΛΦΑ*, AMSTEL-*ΑΜΣΤΕΛ*) is good and very refreshing as it is always served ice-cold. You can also find a variety of foreign brands.

Oózo (**Oózo** – *OYZO*)
Oózo is the most popular Greek aperitif. It is a strong spirit with an aniseed flavour, distilled from grapes. You can drink it neat or add water, which will make it cloudy. It is served with **meze*th*áki** (titbits) such as olives, a piece of cheese etc. In the villages, they might think you sissy, if you add water to your oozo.

Wines
Wine is a part of the Greek heritage, it goes back to legend, to Dionysus, the God of Wine and Mirth. There is a wide choice of local wines, dry, sweet, light and heavy.

Retsina (*ΡΕΤΣΙΝΑ*), the national drink, is a golden resinated wine, which has an acquired rather than an immediate appeal. As it comes from many parts of the country it varies a lot in quality and is usually better from the barrel than bottled. Retsina can also be red in colour and then it is called **kokkinelli**. If you cannot get used to the taste ask for a non-resinated (**aretsínoto** – ἀρετσίνωτο) wine like:

Deméstica, both red and white.

Kambá, a rather dry white wine.

St Hélena, Sánta Láura, very pleasant white, red and rosé wines from the Peloponnese.

Sámos wines, (favoured by Lord Byron) are rich and strong.

Mavrodáphne, red and sweet, good for a dessert wine.

There are many, many more and they are cheap to buy, so be adventurous try a lot and decide for yourself, which you favour . . . .

Brandies and cognacs

There are several brandies, some of which are very good. Probably the best known, is **'Metaxas'** with a rich, fruity flavour.

Soft drinks

I'd like . . . please	**parakaló thélo** Παρακαλῶ θέλω
– chocolate	– **mía sokoláta** – μια σοκολάτα
plain	**skéti** σκέτη
with cream	**me kréma** μέ κρέμα
– cocoa	– **éna kakáo** – ἕνα κακάο
– coffee	– **éna kafé** – ἕνα καφέ
Greek	**elinikó** ἑλληνικό
French	**ghalikó** γαλλικό
espresso	**expréso** εξπρέσσο
frappé	**'frappé'** φραπέ
instant	**nescafé** νεσκαφέ
iced	**paghoméno** παγωμενο
black	**skéto** σκέτο
with cream/milk	**me kréma/ghála** μέ κρέμα/ γάλα

– lemonade (fizzy)   – **mía gazóza** – μία γκαζόζα
– lemonade (juice)   – **mía lemonátha me lemóni**
                        – μία λεμονάδα μέ λεμόνι
– orangeade   – **mía portokalátha** – μία
                          πορτοκαλάδα
– orangeade (juice)   – **mía portokalátha me portokáli**
                        – μία πορτοκαλάδα μέ πορτοκάλι
– milk   – **ghála** – γάλα
– milk shake   – **'milk shake'** – 'μιλκ σέΐκ
– soda water   – **mía sótha** – μία σόδα
– tea   – **éna tsái** – ἕνα τσάι
   with milk/lemon   **me ghála/lemóni** μέ γάλα/
                           λεμόνι
– vissinátha (a soft drink made – **mía visinátha** – μία βισσινάδα
   from morello cherries)
– water   – **neró** – νερό
   iced   **paghoméno** παγωμένο
   mineral (bottled)   **botilyarisméno**
                           μποτιλιαρισμένο
   with sugar   **me záhari** μέ ζάχαρη
   without sugar   **horís záhari** χωρις ζάχαρη

Note: Mineral water is usually asked for by its brand name, *e.g.*
Sáriza, Ívi, Karandáni, Lootrakíoo etc.

Note: The most usual ways of ordering Greek coffee are:
(a) **skétos**   no sugar
(b) **métrios**   medium sweet
(c) **varís ghlikós**   strong and sweet

VOCABULARY

Meat   **Kréas** κρέας
beef   **moshári** μοσχάρι
chicken   **kotópoolo** κοτόπουλο
kid   **katsikáki** κατσικάκι
lamb   **arnáki** ἀρνάκι

pork	**hirinó** χοιρινό
veal	**mosharáki** μοσχαράκι
liver	**sikóti** συκώτι
kidneys	**nefrá** νεφρά
chops	**brizóles** μπριζόλες
cutlets	**paithákia** παϊδάκια
minced meat	**kimás** κιμᾶς
steak	**filéto** φιλέτο
fillet steak	**bon filé** μπόν φιλέ
Without fat please	**horís páhos parakaló** χωρίς πάχος παρακαλῶ

Fish	**Psári** ψάρι
cod	**bakaliáros** μπακαλιάρος
grey mullet	**lithríni** λιθρίνι
lobster	**astakós** ἀστακός
mackerel	**kolyós** κολιός
mussels	**míthya** μύδια
octopus	**htapóthi** χταπόδι
oysters	**stríthya** στρείδια
prawns	**gharíthes** γαρίδες
red mullet	**barboóni** μπαρμπούνι
sardine	**sarthéla** σαρδέλλα
sardine (large)	**ghópa** γόπα
sole	**ghlósa** γλῶσσα
sprats	**marítha** μαρίδα
smelts	**maritháki** μαριδάκι
squid	**kalamaráki** καλαμαράκι
swordfish	**ksifías** ξιφίας
snapper	**tsipoóra** τσιπούρα

Vegetables	**Lahaniká** λαχανικά
artichokes	**aghináres** ἀγκινάρες
aubergines	**melidzánes** μελιτζάνες
cabbage	**láhano** λάχανο
carrots	**karóta** καρότα
cauliflower	**koonoopíthi** κουνουπίδι
celery	**sélino** σέλινο

courgettes	**kolokithákya** *κολοκυθάκια*
cucumber	**agoóri** *ἀγγούρι*
garlic	**skórt*h*o** *σκόρδο*
greens	**hórta** *χόρτα*
greens (wild)	**rat*h*íkya** *ραδίκια*
ladies' fingers	**bámyes** *μπάμιες*
lemon	**lemóni** *λεμόνι*
lettuce	**mɑroóli** *μαρούλι*
onions	**kremít*h*ya** *κρεμμύδια*
peppers	**piperiés** *πιπεριές*
potatoes	**patátes** *πατάτες*
radishes	**rapanákya** *ραπανάκια*
spinach	**spanáki** *σπανάκι*
tomatoes	**domátes** *ντομάτες*

Fruit	**Froóta** *φροῦτα*
apples	**míla** *μῆλα*
apricots	**veríkoka** *βερύκοκα*
bananas	**banánes** *μπανάνες*
cherries	**kerásya** *κεράσια*
figs	**síka** *σῦκα*
grapes	**stafílya** *σταφύλια*
grapefruit	**'grapefruit'** *γκρέϊπ φρούτ*
melon	**pepóni** *πεπόνι*
oranges	**portokálya** *πορτοκάλια*
peaches	**rot*h*ákina** *ροδάκινα*
pears	**ahlát*h*ya** *ἀχλάδια*
plums	**t*h*amáskina** *δαμάσκηνα*
strawberries	**fráooles** *φράουλες*
tangerines	**mandarínya** *μανταρίνια*
water melon	**karpoózi** *καρπούζι*

Suggestion: You must try, if you are in the country during August:

fresh almonds	**fréska míght*h*ala** *φρέσκα μύγδαλα*

fresh walnuts	**fréska karíthya** *φρέσκα καρύδια*

'Pass-the-time' favourites (especially when watching a film in the open-air cinema):

roasted pumpkin seeds	**pasatémpos** *πασσατέμπος*
roasted chick-peas	**straghálya** *στραγάλια*
roasted pistachio nuts	**fistíkia** *φιστίκια*

The menu

Here is a list of the main headings on a Greek menu, together with a few Greek specialities that you might like to try.

ΌΡΕΚΤΙΚΑ **orektiká** *(Μεζέδες)* **(mezethes)**	*APPETISERS*
Ταραμοσαλάτα **taramosaláta**	a paté of smoked cod's roe blended with bread, olive oil and vinegar or lemon
Μελιτζανοσαλάτα **melidzanosaláta**	Aubergine baked on charcoal mashed and mixed with olive oil and lemon
Ντολμάδες γιαλαντζή **dolmáthes yalandzí**	Vine leaves stuffed with rice and dill
Καλαμαράκια **kalamarákia**	Young squid excellent when small and crisply fried
Χταπόδι στό κάρβουνο **htapóthi sto kárvoono**	Octopus grilled on charcoal
Σατζίκι **sadzíki**	A paté of yogurt, cucumber, garlic
ΣΟΥΠΕΣ **soópes**	*SOUPS*
Σούπα αὐγολέμονο **soópa avgholémono**	Egg and lemon soup with rice

Χορτόσουπα **hortósoopa**	Vegetable soup
Ψαρόσουπα **psarósoopa**	Fish soup
Μαγειρίτσα **mayirítsa**	Egg and lemon soup with minced lamb and entrails (A traditional Easter soup)
Φασολάδα **fasolátha**	Kidney bean soup with onions and carrots and celery (often eaten as a main course)
Πατσᾶς **patsás**	Tripe soup

ZYMAPIKA **zimariká** — *PASTA, RICE, PIES*

Μακαρόνια μέ κυμᾶ **makarónia me kimá**	Spaghetti with minced meat sauce
Παστίτσιο μέ κυμᾶ **pastítsio me kimá**	Macaroni with minced meat rolled in filo and baked in the oven (Filo is a paper-thin pastry used in most Greek pies.)
Τυρόπιτα **tirópita**	Cheese pie made with filo
Πιλάφι **piláfi**	Pilaf (rice)

ΘΑΛΑΣΣΙΝΑ **thalasiná** — *SEA FOOD*

Μαριδάκι **maritháki**	Fried smelt
Γαρίδες λαδολέμονο **gharíthes latholémono**	Prawns in oil and lemon sauce
Χταπόδι κρασάτο **htapóthi krasáto**	Octopus stewed in red wine
Μπαρμπούνια τῆς σχάρας τηγανητά **barboónia tis sháras tighanitá**	Red mullet grilled fried
Μπακαλιάρος μέ σκορδαλιά **bakaliáros me skorthalyá**	Fried salt cod with strong garlic sauce

Ψάρι πλακί
psári plakí
Ψάρι στό χαρτί
psári sto hartí

Fish stewed with onions, tomatoes, herbs and vegetables

Fish baked in grease-proof paper

Note: For more types of fish and seafood see fish list in food section.

ΛΑΔΕΡΑ
latherá

COOKED IN OIL

Μπάμιες γιαχνί
bámyes yahní
'Αγκινάρες αλά πολίτα
angináres a la políta

Melιτζάνες ιμάμ μπαϊλντί
melidzánes imám baildí

Γεμιστές ντομάτες
yemistés domátes

Ladies fingers (okra) braised in oil with tomatoes and onions

Artichokes cooked in oil and lemon juice with spring onion and dill

Aubergines cooked in oil and stuffed with tomatoes, garlic, onions and parsley

Stuffed tomatoes with rice, onion, parsley (currants)

Note: **Latherá**, usually served cold, can be delicious and so filling that often they are used as the main course, although they contain no meat.

ΨΗΤΑ
psitá
'Αρνάκι σούβλας
arnáki soóvlas
Κοκορέτσι
kokorétsi

ROASTS AND GRILLS

Lamb roast on a spit

Spiced pieces of heart, liver and kidney, lashed with strips of entrail, to a skewer and grilled

ΕΝΤΡΑΔΕΣ
entráthes
Μουσακᾶς
moosakás

ENTRÉES

Layers of sliced aubergine and minced meat covered with cheese sauce, baked in the oven

Γιουβέτσι **gioovétsi**	Meat with spaghetti and tomatoes baked in the oven
Ντολμάδες **dolmáthes**	Minced meat, rice and spices wrapped in vine or cabbage leaves with egg and lemon sauce
Παπουτσάκια **papootsákia**	Marrow or aubergines stuffed with mince meat, rice, onions, covered with cheese sauce and baked
Σουτζουκάκια **sootzookákia**	Meat balls with rice in tomato or egg and lemon sauce
Στιφάδο **stifátho**	A stew of rabbit or hare cooked in oil, wine, small onions
Ἀρνάκι φρικασσέ **arnáki frikasé**	Lamb cooked with lettuce hearts and spring onions with egg and lemon sauce

ΤΗΣΩΡΑΣ / **tis óras** — *GRILLS WHILE YOU WAIT*

Σουβλάκια **soovlákia**	Pieces of meat, tomato, onion, grilled on skewers (kebabs)
Κεφτέδες σχάρας **keftéthes sháras**	Grilled meat balls
Μπόν-φιλέ **bon-filé**	Steak (best cut)
Παϊδάκια ἀρνίσια **paithákia arnísia**	Lamb cutlets
Μπριζόλες **brizóles**	Chops
Μοσχαρίσιες **mosharísies**	Veal
Χοιρινές **hirinés**	Pork
Φιλέτο σχάρας **filéto sháras**	Grilled steak

ΣΑΛΑΤΕΣ	*SALADS*
salàtes	
Χωριάτικη σαλάτα	Tomatoes, green pepper, fetta
horiátiki saláta	cheese, olives
Ντοματοσαλάτα	Tomatoes with onions or
domatosaláta	cucumbers, green pepper
Ραδίκια ἄγρια	Bitter, wild mountain greens,
rathíkia ághria (wild)	boiled and served with an oil
	and lemon dressing

Note: Most salads are served with an oil and vinegar dressing. Usually there is a lot of oil. If you don't like it say:

– A little oil	**lígho láthi**
	λίγο λάδι
– Without oil	**horís láthi**
	χωρίς λάδι
– Plain salad without oil and	**skéti saláta horís lathóksitho**
vinegar	*σκέτη σαλάτα χωρίς λαδόξυδο*

ΤΥΡΙΑ	*CHEESES*
tiryá	
Φέτα	A white cheese made from goat's
féta	milk
Κασέρι	A yellow firm cheese, mildly
kaséri	flavoured
Μανούρι	A sweet soft cheese
manoóri	
Γραβιέρα ἑλληνική	The Greek version of gruyere,
ghraviéra ellinikí	made from ewe's milk
Μυζήθρα	A soft cottage cheese
mizíthra	

Note: **Féta** is the most popular cheese in Greece but it varies widely from place to place. It can be hard or crumbly or very salty. It can be extremely good to eat or at its worst it can taste like a piece of salty chalk.

ΓΛΥΚΙΣΜΑΤΑ (ΓΛΥΚΑ)　　**DESSERTS**
ghlikísmata gliká)

Μπακλαβᾶς	Walnuts, almonds soaked in
baklavás	honey and wrapped in flaky
	pastry (filo)
Γαλακτομπούρεκο	Fine pastry (filo) with a custard
ghalaktoboóreko	filling
Καταῖφι	Walnuts, almonds and honey
kataífi	bound by shredded pastry
Λουκουμάδες	Honey puffs, made of a yeast
lookoomáthes	mixture, powdered with
	cinnamon and dipped in honey
Ριζόγαλο	Greek rice pudding usually served
rizóghalo	cold

Note: Greek pastry **(filo)** is a plain paper-thin pastry used in most Greek pastries and pies.

Generally speaking, Greeks do not finish a meal with a sweet. More often than not you'll have to go to a **ghalaktopolion** (dairy shop) or to a **zaharoplastion** (pastry shop) for your dessert.

Restaurants, Cafés and Bars

Reserving and getting a table

Can you recommend a good and not very expensive restaurant?

mípos ksérete kanéna kaló ke óhi akrivó restorán (estiatório)

Μήπως ξέρετε κανένα καλό κι ὄχι ἀκριβό ρεστωράν; (ἐστιατόριο);

I'd like to book a table for four at 8 tonight.

thélo na kratíso éna trapézi ya (4) téseris stis (8) októ to vráthi

Θέλω νά κρατήσω ἕνα τραπέζι γιά τέσσερεις στίς (8) ὀκτώ τό βράδυ.

*Yes, fine.

málista, endáksi

Μάλιστα, ἐντάξει.

*Your name please?

ti ónoma parakaló

Τί ὄνομα παρακαλῶ;

*Can you come earlier/later?

boríte na élthete norítera/arghótera

Μπορεῖτε νά ἔλθετε νωρίτερα/ἀργότερα;

*Sorry, we are all booked up, tonight.

óhi, then éhome trapézi ya apópse

Ὄχι, δέν ἔχομε τραπέζι γιά ἀπόψε.

My name is Mr Smith, I have reserved a table for four.

íme o kírios Smith,ého kratísi éna trapézi ya (4) téseris

Εἶμαι ὁ κύριος Σμίθ, ἔχω κρατήσει ἕνα τραπέζι γιά (4) τέσσερεις.

Good evening, I'd like a table for two.

kalispéra sas, éhete éna trapézi ya (2) thío

Καλησπέρα σας, ἔχετε ἕνα τραπέζι γιά (2) δύο.

We are in a hurry.	**viazómaste polí**
	Βιαζόμαστε πολύ.
Can you serve us at once?	**boríte na mas servírete amésos**
	Μπορεῖτε νά μᾶς σερβίρετε
	ἀμέσως;
Where is the toilet please?	**poo íne i tooaléta parakaló**
	Ποῦ εἶναι ἡ τουαλέττα,
	παρακαλῶ;

Ordering a meal

Can we have the menu please?	**ton katálogho (menu) parakaló**
	Τόν κατάλογο παρακαλῶ;
Can I have the wine list?	**ton katálogho ton krasión**
	parakaló
	Τόν κατάλογο τῶν κρασιῶν,
	παρακαλῶ;
What is this?	**to íne aftó**
	Τί εἶναι αὐτό;
Is this nice?	**íne kaló**
	Εἶναι καλό;
What do you recommend?	**ti moo sinistáte na páro**
	Τί μοῦ συνιστᾶτε νά πάρω;
Can I see what you have? (in the kitchen)	**boró na tho ti éhete (stin koozína)**
	Μπορῶ νά δῶ τί ἔχετε; (στήν
	κουζίνα)
I'll have	**tha páro**
	Θά πάρω . . . .
What do you serve with the meat/fish?	**ti servírete me to kréas/psári**
	Τί σερβίρετε με τό κρέας/ψάρι;
*How do you like your steak done?	**pos to thélete to biftéki sas**
	Πῶς τό θέλετε τό μπιφτέκι
	σας;
– rare (very)?	**– lígho psiméno (shethón ápsito)**
	– λίγο ψημένο (σχέδον ἄψητο);
– medium?	**– métrio**
	– μέτριο;

– well done?	– **kalopsiméno**
	– *καλοψημένο;*
Bring it with/without	**to thélo me/horís**
	Τό θέλω μέ/χωρίς ....
– sauce.	– **sáltsa**
	– *σάλτσα.*
– garlic.	– **skórtho**
	– *σκόρδο.*
– onion.	– **kremíthi**
	– *κρεμμύδι.*
– oil.	– **láthi**
	– *λάδι.*
Is it hot or cold?	**íne zestó i krío**
	Εἶναι ζεστό ἤ κρύο;
What do you serve with the roast?	**ti servírete me to psitó**
	Τί σερβίρετε μέ τό ψητό;
*There is no more.	**telíose**
	Τελείωσε.

Drinks

What will you drink? (see list of Greek wines)	**ti tha pyíte**
	Τί θά πιῆτε;
I would like	**thélo**
	Θέλω ....
– a bottle of retsina.	– **éna bookáli retsína.**
	– *ἔνα μπουκάλι ρετσίνα.*
– half a bottle of unresinated wine.	– **misó bookáli aretsínoto krasí**
	– *μισό μπουκάλι ἀρετσίνωτο κρασί.*
– a carafe of red wine.	– **mía karáfa kókino krasí**
	– *μιά καράφα κόκκινο κρασί.*
– a glass of white wine.	– **éna potíri krasí áspro**
	– *ἔνα ποτῆρι κρασί ἄσπρο.*
– a litre of rosé.	– **éna lítro rozé**
	– *ἔνα λίτρο ροζέ.*
I would like	**thélo**
	Θέλω ....

– an (iced) beer.	**– mía (paghoméni) bíra** *– μιά (παγωμένη) μπύρα.*
– a fizzy lemonade.	**– mía gazóza** *– μιά γκαζόζα.*
– a (cold) lemonade.	**– mía (kría) lemonátha** *– μιά (κρύα) λεμονάδα.*
– cold water.	**– krío neró** *– κρύο νερό.*
Please could you boil some milk for the child?	**parakaló borite ná vrásete lígho ghála ya to pethí** *Παρακαλῶ μπορεῖτε νά βράσετε λίγο γάλα γιά τό παιδί;*
Please bring some more bread.	**férte lígho akómi psomí, pavakoló** *Φέρτε λίγο ἀκόμη ψωμί, παρακαλῶ.*
Please bring some more wine.	**férte lígho akómi krasí, parakoló** *Φέρτε λίγο ἀκόμη κρασί, παρακαλῶ.*
Cheers	**stin iyiásas** *Στήν ὑγειά σας*

Complaints

This isn't what I ordered.	**then to paríngila aftó** *Δέν τό παρήγγειλα αὐτό.*
I have ordered	**paríngila** *Παρήγγειλα . . . .*
This is	**aftó íne** *Αὐτό εἶναι . . . .*
– dirty.	**– vrómiko** *– βρώμικο.*
– uncooked.	**– ápsito** *– ἄψητο.*
– stale.	**– bayiátiko** *– μπαγιάτικο.*
– bad (off).	**– halasméno** *– χαλασμένο.*
This has too much fat.	**éhi poli páhos** *Ἔχει πολύ πάχος.*
May I change this?	**boríte na to aláksete** *Μπορεῖτε νά τό ἀλλάξετε;*

I'd like to see the manager.	**thélo na *th*o ton ipéfthino**
	Θέλω νά δῶ τόν ὑπεύθυνο.

Paying the bill

cover charge	**koovér**
	Κουβέρ
service charge (tip)	**posostó servitóron (filo*th*órima)**
	Ποσοστό σερβιτόρων
	(φιλοδώρημα)
tip	**filothórima (pour-boir)**
	Φιλοδώρημα (πούρ-μπουάρ)
Can I have the bill please?	**ton logharyasmó parakaló**
	Τόν λογαριασμό, παρακαλῶ;
May we have separate bills please?	**horistoós logharyasmoós, parakaló**
	Χωριστούς λογαρια-σμούς, παρακαλῶ;
I think there is a mistake.	**nomízo óti éhete éna láthos**
	Νομίζω ὅτι ἔχετε ἕνα λάθος.
I didn't have	***th*en píra**
	Δέν πῆρα . . . .
I didn't order	***th*en paríngila**
	Δέν παρήγγειλα . . . .
We had only one salad.	**pírame móno (1) mía saláta**
	Πήραμε μόνο (1) μιά σαλάτα.
Is service included?	**íne mésa ke to filo*th*órima**
	Εἶναι μέσα καί τό φιλοδώρημα;
This is for you. (tip to the waiter)	**aftó íne ya sas**
	Αὐτό εἶναι γιά σᾶς.
This is for the young boy.	**aftó ya ton mikró**
	Αὐτό γιά τόν μικρό.
It was a very good meal.	**polí oréo to fayitó**
	Πολύ ὡραῖο τό φαγητό.
Thank you, Good-bye.	**efharistó, andío**
	Εὐχαριστῶ, ἀντίο.

Note: Even when service is included, one still tips the waiter and the young boy who helps him.

VOCABULARY

I'd like a(n) (the)	tha íthela Θά ἤθελα ....
– ashtray	– éna tasáki – ἕνα τασάκι
– till	– ton logharyasmó – τόν λογαριασμό
– bottle	– éna bookáli – ἕνα μπουκάλι
– chair	– mía karékla – μιά καρέκλα
– corkscrew	– éna tirboosón – ἕνα τιρμπουσόν
– cup	– éna flitzáni – ἕνα φλυτζάνι
– egg-cup	– mía avghothíki – μιά αὐγοθήκη
– fork	– éna piroóni – ἕνα πιρούνι
– glass	– éna potíri – ἕνα ποτῆρι
– helping	– mía merítha – μία μερίδα
– knife	– éna mahéri – ἕνα μαχαίρι
– menu	– ton katálogho – τόν κατάλογο
– napkin	– mía petséta – μιά πετσέτα
– plate	– éna pyáto – ἕνα πιᾶτο
– spoon	– éna kootáli – ἕνα κουτάλι
– tea-spoon	– éna kootaláki – ἕνα κουταλάκι
The waiter	– to garsón (o servitóros) τό γκαρσόν (ὁ σερβιτόρος)
The waiter's assistant	o mikrós ὁ μικρός

I'd like	thélo Θέλω ....
– oil and vinegar	– lathóksitho – λαδόξυδο
– ketchup	– kétchup – κετσάπ
– mustard	– moostártha – μουστάρδα
– pepper	– pipéri – πιπέρι
– salt	– aláti – ἁλάτι
– coffee	– kafé – καφέ
– milk	– ghála – γάλα
– sugar	– záhari – ζάχαρη
– tea	– tsái – τσάϊ
– ice-cream	– paghotó – παγωτό
– lemonade	– lemonátha – λεμονάδα
– lemonade (fizzy)	– gazóza – γκαζόζα
– orangeade	– portokalátha – πορτοκαλάδα

| – water | – neró | – νερό |
| – wine | – krasí | – κρασί |

Methods of cooking

Baked (cooked in the oven)	sto foórno	στό φοῦρνο
Baked in parchment (in the oven)	eksohikó sto hartí	ἐξοχικό στό χαρτί
Boiled	vrastó	βραστό
Fried	tighanitó	τηγανητό
Grilled	tis sháras	τῆς σχάρας
On charcoal	sto kárvoono	στό κάρβουνο
On the spit	sti soóvla	στή σούβλα
Pot-roasted	psitó tis katsarólas	ψητό τῆς κατσαρόλας
Roasted	psitó	ψητό
Smoked	kapnistó	καπνιστό
Stewed	yahní	γιαχνί
Stuffed	yemistá	γεμιστά

Loss or Theft

Someone has stolen my . . . .
moo klépsane
Μοῦ κλέψανε . . . .

– passport.
– to thiavatirio moo
– τό διαβατήριό μου.

– driving licence.
– tin áthia othiyíseos
– τήν ἄδεια ὁδηγήσεως.

– insurance certificate.
– to pistopiitikó asfalíseos
– τό πιστοποιητικό ἀσφαλίσεως.

– car keys.
– ta klithiá too aftokinítoo moo
– τά κλειδιά τοῦ αὐτοκινήτου μου.

– car papers.
– ta hartyá too aftokinítoo moo
– τά χαρτιά τοῦ αὐτοκινήτου μου.

– money.
– ta leptá moo
– τά λεπτά μου.

– traveller's cheques.
– ta 'traveller's cheques'
– τά τράβελερς τσέκς.

– credit card.
– tin 'credit card' (pistotikí kárta)
– τήν κρέντιτ κάρντ (πιστωτική κάρτα).

– ticket (plane).
– to isitirió moo (aeroporikó)
– τό εἰσιτήριό μου (ἀεροπορικό).

I have lost my . . . .
éhasa
Ἔχασα . . . .

– camera.
– tin fotoghrafikí mihaní moo
– τήν φωτογραφική μηχανή μου.

– wallet.
– to portofóli moo
– τό πορτοφόλι μου.

– jewellery.
– ta kosmímata moo
– τά κοσμήματα μου.

– handbag.

    – tin tsánda moo
    – τήν τσάντα μου.

– briefcase.

    – ton hartofilaka moo
    – τόν χαρτοφύλακα μου.

*When did you lose it?

    póte to hasate
    Πότε τό χάσατε;

*Where did you lose it?

    poó to hasate
    Ποῦ τό χάσατε;

It was in . . . .

    ítane mésa
    Ἤτανε μέσα . . . .

– my car.

    – sto aftokínito moo
    – στό αὐτοκίνητο μου.

– my room.

    – sto *th*omátio moo
    – στό δωμάτιο μου.

– my cabin.

    – stin cabína moo
    – στήν καμπίνα μου.

– I lost it in the street.

    – to éhasa sto *th*rómo
    – Τό ἔχασα στό δρόμο.

LOST PROPERTY

14 Messoghion (*ΜΕΣΟΓΕΙΩΝ*)
  Street

           7705–711

In taxis or buses: Traffic Police
  (**trohéa**) Ag. Konstantinou (*ΑΓ.*
  ΚΩΝΣΤΑΝΤΙΝΟΥ) Street

           5230-111 ext. 120

Reference Section

Numbers

	(M)(F)(N)		
1	**énas mía** *éna* ἔνας, μία, ἔνα		
2	**thío** δύο		
3	**tris** *tría* τρεῖς, τρεῖς, τρία		
4	**téseris téseris** *tésera* τέσσερεις, τέσσερεις, τέσσερα		
5	**pénde** πέντε		
6	**éksi** ἔξη		
7	**eptá** ἑπτά		
8	**októ** ὀκτώ		
9	**enéa** ἐννέα		
10	**théka** δέκα		
11	**éntheka** ἔνδεκα		
12	**thótheka** δώδεκα		
13	**thekatría** δεκατρία		
14	**thekatésera** δεκατέσσερα		
15	**thekapénde** δεκαπέντε		
16	**thekaéksi** δεκαέξι		
17	**thekaeptá** δεκαεπτά		
18	**thekaoktó** δεκαοκτώ		
19	**thekaenéa** δεκαεννέα		
20	**íkosi** εἴκοσι		
21	**ikosiéna** εἰκοσιένα		
22	**ikosithío** εἰκοσιδύο		
23	**ikositría** εἰκοσιτρία		
24	**ikositésera** εἰκοσιτέσσερα		
25	**ikosipénde** εἰκοσιπέντε		
26	**ikosiéksi** εἰκοσιέξη		

27	**ikosieptá**	εἰκοσιεπτά
28	**ikosioktó**	εἰκοσιοκτώ
29	**ikosienéa**	εἰκοσιεννέα
30	**triánda**	τριάντα
40	**saránda**	σαράντα
50	**penínda**	πενήντα
60	**eksínda**	ἑξήντα
70	**ev*th*omínda**	ἑβδομήντα
80	**ogh*th*ónda**	ὀγδόντα
90	**enenínda**	ἐνενήντα
100	**ekató**	ἑκατό
101	**ekatón éna**	ἑκατόν ἕνα
102	**ekatón *th*ío**	ἑκατόν δύο
150	**ekatón penínda**	ἑκατόν πενήντα
200	***th*iakósia**	διακόσια
250	***th*iakósia penínda**	διακόσια πενήντα
300	**triakósia**	τριακόσια
400	**tetrakósia**	τετρακόσια
500	**pendakósia**	πεντακόσια
600	**eksakósia**	ἑξακόσια
700	**eptakósia**	ἑπτακόσια
800	**oktakósia**	ὀκτακόσια
900	**enyakósia**	ἐννιακόσια
1000	**hília**	χίλια
1500	**hília pendakósia**	χίλια πεντακόσια
2000	***th*ío hiliáthes**	δύο χιλιάδες
10.000	***th*éka hiliáthes**	δέκα χιλιάδες
100.000	**ekató hiliáthes**	ἑκατό χιλιάδες
1.000.000	**éna ekatomírio**	ἕνα ἑκατομμύριο
1.000.000.000	**éna *th*isekatomírio**	ἕνα δισεκατομμύριο

Note: The comma (,) in Greek is used for decimal numbers only.

0	**mi*th*én**	μηδέν
¼	**to ena tétarto**	τό ἕνα τέταρτο
½	**to misó**	τό μισό
⅓	**to éna tríto**	τό ἕνα τρίτο

⅔	**ta *th*ío tríta**	τά δύο τρίτα
a dozen	**mía *thoth*ekátha**	μία δωδεκάδα
double	**to *th*iplásio**	τό διπλάσιο

Combination of numbers

131	**ekatón triánda éna**
	Έκατόν τριάντα ἕνα
372	**triakósia evthomínda *th*ío**
	Τριακόσια ἑβδομήντα δύο
1.250	**hília *th*iakósia peнínda**
	Χίλια διακόσια πενήντα
1980	**hília enyakósia ogh*th*ónda**
	Χίλια ἐννιακόσια ὀγδόντα

Ordinal numbers

	(M)	(F)	(N)
first	**prótos**	**próti**	**próto**
	Πρῶτος	πρώτη	πρῶτο
second	**théfteros**	**théfteri**	**théftero**
	Δεύτερος	δεύτερη	δεύτερο
third	**trítos**	**tríti**	**tríto**
	Τρίτος	τρίτη	τρίτο
fourth	**tétartos**	**tetárti**	**tétarto**
	Τέταρτος	τετάρτη	τέταρτο
fifth	**pémptos**	**pémpti**	**pémpto**
	Πέμπτος	πέμπτη	πέμπτο
sixth	**éktos**	**ékti**	**ékto**
	Έκτος	ἕκτη	ἕκτο
seventh	**év*th*omos**	**ev*th*ómi**	**év*th*omo**
	Έβδομος	ἑβδόμη	ἕβδομο
eighth	**ógh*th*oos**	**ogh*th*ói**	**ógh*th*oo**
	Όγδοος	ὀγδόη	ὄγδοο
ninth	**énatos**	**enáti**	**énato**
	Έννατος	ἐννάτη	ἕννατο
tenth	**thékatos**	**thekáti**	**thékato**
	Δέκατος	δεκάτη	δέκατο

once	**mía forá**
	Μία φορά
twice	**thío forés**
	Δύο φορές
three times	**tris forés**
	Τρεῖς φορές
a thousand times	**hílies forés**
	Χίλιες φορές
infinite times	**ápires forés**
	Ἄπειρες φορές
more	**perisótero**
	Περισσότερο
less	**lighótero**
	Λιγότερο
a lot	**polí**
	Πολύ
a little	**lígho**
	Λίγο
a few	**meriká**
	Μερικά

The time

i óra
Ἡ ὥρα

The time is feminine; therefore for numbers 1, 3, 4, we use the feminine form. We say:

One o'clock	**mía**	*Μία*
Three o'clock	**tris**	*Τρεῖς*
Four o'clock	**téseris**	*Τέσσερις*

For the rest of the numbers there is no change. *E.g.*

Five o'clock	**pénde**	*πέντε*
Six o'clock	**éksi etc.** (see list of numbers)	*ἕξι*
Five past one	**mía ke pénde**	
	Μία καί πέντε	

Ten past one	**mía ke *th*éka**
	Μία καί δέκα
quarter past one	**mía ke tétarto**
	Μία καί τέταρτο
Twenty past one	**mía ke íkosi**
	Μία καί εἴκοσι
Twenty five past one	**mía ke íkosi pénde**
	Μία καί εἴκοσι πέντε
half past one	**mía ke misí**
	Μία καί μισή
Twenty five to two	***th*ío pará íkosi pénde**
	Δύο παρά εἴκοσι πέντε
Twenty to two	***th*ío pará íkosi**
	Δύο παρά εἴκοσι
quarter to two	***th*ío pará tétarto**
	Δύο παρά τέταρτο
Ten to two	***th*ío pará *th*éka**
	Δύο παρά δέκα
Five to two	***th*ío pará pénde**
	Δύο παρά πέντε
Two o'clock	***th*ío**
	Δύο
What time is it?	**tí óra íne**
	Τί ὥρα εἶναι;
Have you got the time please?	**éhete óra parakaló**
	Ἔχετε ὥρα παρακαλῶ;
It's seven (exactly).	**íne eptá (akrivós)**
	Εἶναι ἐπτά (ἀκριβῶς).
It's (nearly) ten.	**íne (perípoo) *th*éka**
	Εἶναι (περίπου) δέκα.

Some time phrases

I'll see you at	**tha se *th*o**
	Θά σέ δῶ . . . .
– ten in the morning.	**– stis (10) *th*éka to proí**
	– στίς δέκα τό πρωί.

– eight in the evening.

– stis (8) októ to vráthi
– στίς ὀκτώ τό βράδυ.

– midday.

– to mesiméri
– τό μεσημέρι.

– midnight.

– ta mesánikta
– τά μεσάνυκτα.

I'm sorry I'm late.

me sinhoríte poo áryisa
Μέ συγχωρεῖτε πού ἄργησα.

I'm afraid I'm early.

fováme pos írtha norís
Φοβᾶμαι πῶς ἦρθα νωρίς.

*You have plenty of time.

éhete polí óra akómi
Ἔχετε πολλή ὥρα ἀκόμη.

*You have no time.

then éhete keró
Δέν ἔχετε καιρό.

It's time we left.

íne óra na fíghoome
Εἶναι ὥρα νά φύγωμε.

How long does it take?

rósi óra tha pári
Πόση ὥρα θά πάρει;

A minute.

éna leptó
Ἕνα λεπτό.

A few minutes.

meriká leptá
Μερικά λεπτά.

One hour.

mía óra
Μία ὥρα.

Half an hour.

misí óra
Μισή ὥρα.

My watch is slow.

to rolói moo pái píso
Τό ρολόϊ μου πάει πίσω.

My watch is fast.

to rolói moo pái brostá
Τό ρολόϊ μου πάει μπροστά.

Don't be late.

min aryísete
Μήν ἀργήσετε.

Wait a minute.

periménete éna leptó
Περιμένετε ἕνα λεπτό.

It's late.

íne arghá
Εἶναι ἀργά.

It's early.   **íne norís**
         Εἶναι νωρίς.

He is late.   **áryise**
         Ἄργησε.

He is early.   **írthe norís**
         Ἦρθε νωρίς.

Hurry up.   **káne ghríghora**
         Κάνε γρήγορα.

Days of the week
Sunday   **i kiriakí** *ἡ Κυριακή*
Monday   **i theftéra** *ἡ Δευτέρα*
Tuesday   **i tríti** *ἡ Τρίτη*
Wednesday   **i tetárti** *ἡ Τετάρτη*
Thursday   **i pémpti** *ἡ Πέμπτη*
Friday   **i paraskeví** *ἡ Παρασκευή*
Saturday   **to sávato** *τό Σάββατο*

Today   **símera** *Σήμερα*
Tomorrow   **ávrio** *Αὔριο*
The day after tomorrow **methávrio** *Μεθαύριο*
Yesterday   **hthés** *Χθές*
The day before yesterday **prohthés** *Προχθές*
Every day   **káthe méra** *Κάθε μέρα*
All day   **óli tin iméra** *Ὅλη τήν ἡμέρα*
Three days ago   **prin apó tris méres** *Πρίν ἀπό*
           τρεῖς μέρες
In five days' time   **se pénde méres** *Σέ πέντε μέρες*
The day   **i iméra** *Ἡ ἡμέρα*
The night   **i níkta** *Ἡ νύκτα*
The week   **i evthomátha** *Ἡ ἑβδομάδα*
Last week   **tin perasméni evthomátha** *Τήν*
          περασμένη ἑβδομάδα
Next week   **tin áli evthomátha** *Τήν ἄλλη*
          ἑβδομάδα
A week today   **símera októ** *Σήμερα ὀκτώ*
What day is it today? **ti méra íne símera**
         Τί μέρα εἶναι σήμερα;

When is your birthday?
póte íne ta yenéthliá soo
Πότε εἶναι τά γενέθλιά σου;

When is your name day?
póte íne i yortí soo
Πότε εἶναι ἡ γιορτή σου;

Is it a holiday today?
éhi aryía símera
Ἔχει ἀργία σήμερα;

When do you have your holidays?
póte éhis *th*iakopés
Πότε ἔχεις διακοπές;

I'll see you at the weekend
tha se *th*ó to savatokíriako
Θά σέ δῶ τό Σαββατοκύριακο

I'll see you on Tuesday.
tha se *th*o tin Tríti
Θά σέ δῶ τήν Τρίτη.

I'll see you in a . . . .
tha se *th*o
Θά σέ δῶ . . . .

– week.
– semiá ev*th*omátha
– σέμιά ἔβδομάδα

– fortnight.
– se *th*ío ev*th*omáthes
– σέ δύο ἐβδομάδες.

– month.
– séna mína
– σ᾽ ἕνα μῆνα.

– a year.
– too hrónoo
– τοῦ χρόνου.

The months

January	**ianooários**	*Ἰανουάριος*
February	**fevrooários**	*Φεβρουάριος*
March	**mártios**	*Μάρτιος*
April	**aprílios**	*Ἀπρίλιος*
May	**máios**	*Μάιος*
June	**iónios**	*Ἰούνιος*
July	**ioólios**	*Ἰούλιος*
August	**ávghoostos**	*Αὔγουστος*
September	**septémvrios**	*Σεπτέμβριος*
October	**októvrios**	*Ὀκτώβριος*
November	**noémvrios**	*Νοέμβριος*
December	***th*ekémvrios**	*Δεκέμβριος*

In May	**ton máio**
	Τόν Μάϊο
Next March	**ton erhómeno mártio**
	Τόν ἐρχόμενο Μάρτιο
Last June	**ton perasméno ioónio**
	Τόν περασμένο Ἰούνιο
At the end of July	**sta téli too ioolíoo**
	Στά τέλη τοῦ Ἰουλίου
*How long have you been here?	**póso keró ísaste ethó**
	Πόσο καιρό εἴσαστε ἐδῶ;
I have been here a month.	**íme ethó éna mína**
	Εἶμαι ἐδῶ ἕνα μῆνα.
*When are you coming back?	**póte tha ksanaérthete**
	Πότε θά ξαναέρθετε;
In three months' time.	**se tris mínes**
	Σέ τρεῖς μῆνες.

The seasons

Winter	**o himónas** *ὁ χειμῶνας*
Spring	**i ániksi** *ἡ ἄνοιξη*
Summer	**to kalokéri** *τό καλοκαίρι*
Autumn	**to fthinóporo** *τό φθινόπωρο*
in spring	**tin ániksi** *τήν ἄνοιξη*
in winter	**ton himóna** *τόν χειμῶνα*
in summer	**to kalokéri** *τό καλοκαίρι*
in autumn	**to fthinóporo** *τό φθινόπωρο*
winter sports	**ta himeriná spór** *τά χειμερινά σπόρ*
spring flowers	**ta aniksiátika looloóthya** *τά ἀνοιξιάτικα λουλούδια*
summer dresses	**ta kalokeriná foostánya** *τά καλοκαιρινά φουστάνια*
autumn rain	**i fthinoporiní vrohí** *ἡ φθινοπωρινή βροχή*

Colours

beige	**bez** μπέζ
black	**mávro** μαῦρο
blue	**ble** μπλέ
brown	**kafé** καφέ
cream	**krem** κρέμ
gold	**hrisó** χρυσό
green	**prásino** πράσινο
grey	**gri** γκρί
mauve	**mov** μώβ
orange	**portokalí** πορτοκαλί
pink	**roz** ρόζ
red	**kókino** κόκκινο
silver	**asimí** ἀσῆμί
white	**áspro** ἄσπρο
yellow	**kítrino** κίτρινο
light	**aniktó** ἀνοικτό
lighter	**pyó aniktó** πιό ἀνοικτό
dark	**skoóro** σκοῦρο
darker	**pyó skoóro** πιό σκοῦρο

Countries

Africa	**í afrikí** ἡ Ἀφρική
Albania	**í alvanía** ἡ Ἀλβανία
America	**i amerikí** ἡ Ἀμερική
Asia	**i asía** ἡ Ἀσία
Australia	**i afstralía** ἡ Αὐστραλία
Austria	**i afstría** ἡ Αὐστρία
Belgium	**to vélyio** τό Βέλγιο
Brazil	**i vrazilía** ἡ Βραζιλία
Bulgaria	**i voolgharía** ἡ Βουλγαρία
Canada	**o kanathás** ὁ Καναδᾶς
China	**i kína** ἡ Κίνα

Cyprus	i kípros ἡ Κύπρος
Czechoslovakia	i tsehoslovakía ἡ Τσεχοσλοβακία
Denmark	i thanía ἡ Δανία
Egypt	i éyiptos ἡ Αἴγυπτος
England	i anglía ἡ ᾿Αγγλία
Finland	i filanthía ἡ Φιλανδία
France	i ghalía ἡ Γαλλία
Germany	i yermanía ἡ Γερμανία
Greece	i elás ἡ ῾Ελλάς
Holland	i olanthía ἡ ῾Ολλανδία
India	i inthíes οἱ ᾿Ινδίες
Ireland	i irlanthía ἡ ᾿Ιρλανδία
Italy	i italía ἡ ᾿Ιταλία
Japan	i iaponía ἡ ᾿Ιαπωνία
Mexico	to méxico τό Μεξικό
New Zealand	i néa zilanthía ἡ Νέα Ζηλανδία
Norway	i norviyía ἡ Νορβηγία
Portugal	i portoghalía ἡ Πορτογαλία
Russia	i rosía ἡ Ρωσσία
Scotland	i skotía ἡ Σκωτία
South Africa	i nótios afrikí ἡ Νότιος ᾿Αφρική
South America	i nótios amerikí ἡ Νότιος ᾿Αμερική
Spain	i ispanía ἡ ᾿Ισπανία
Switzerland	i elvetía ἡ ῾Ελβετία
USA	i inoménes políties amerikís οἱ ῾Ηνωμένες Πολιτεῖες ᾿Αμερικῆς
Wales	i ooalía ἡ Οὐαλλία
*Where do you come from?	apo poo ísthe ᾿Από ποῦ εἶσθε;
From England	apó tin anglía ᾿Από τήν ᾿Αγγλία
From Greece	apó tin elátha ᾿Από τήν ῾Ελλάδα
From the	apó ᾿Από ....
North	ton vorá τόν Βορρᾶ
South	to nóto τό Νότο
East	tin anatolí τήν ᾿Ανατολή
West	tin thísi τήν Δύση

Nationalities

I'm	íme	*Εἶμαι* ....
	(M)	**(F)**
African	**afrikanós**	**afrikanítha**
	Ἀφρικαν-ός	*-ίδα*
American	**americanós**	**americanítha**
	Ἀμερικαν-ός	*-ίδα*
Arab	**áraps**	**áraps**
	Ἄραψ	*Ἄραψ*
Asian	**asiátis**	**asiátisa**
	Ἀσιάτ-ης	*— ισσα*
Australian	**afstralós**	**afstralétha**
	Αὐστραλ-ός	*-ίδα*
Austrian	**afstriakós**	**afstriakí**
	Αὐστριακ-ός	*-ή*
Belgian	**vélghos**	**velghítha**
	Βέλγ-ος	*-ίδα*
Brazilian	**vrazilianós**	**vraziliani**
	Βραζιλιαν-ὸς	*-ή*
Bulgarian	**voólgharos**	**voolgharítha**
	Βούγαρ-ος	*-ίδα*
Canadian	**kanathós**	**kanathí**
	Καναδ-ός	*-ή*
Chinese	**kinézos**	**kinéza**
	Κινέζ-ος	*-α*
Cypriot	**kíprios**	**kipría**
	Κύπρι-ος	*-α*
Czech	**tsekoslovákos**	**tsekoslováka**
	Τσεχοσλοβάκ-ος	*-α*
Danish	**thanós**	**thanéza**
	Δαν-ός	*-έζα*
Egyptian	**eyíptios**	**eyiptía**
	Αἰγύπτι-ος	*-α*
English	**ánglos**	**anglítha**
	Ἄγγλ-ος	*-ίδα*
Finnish	**filanthós**	**filanthéza**
	Φιλλανδ-ός	*-έζα*

Nationalities

French	ghálos	ghalítha
	Γάλλ-ος	-ίδα
German	ghermanós	ghermanítha
	Γερμαν-ός	-ίδα
Greek	élinas	elinítha
	Έλλην-ας	-ίδα
Dutch	olanthós	olanthéza
	Όλλανδ-ός	-έζα
Indian	inthós	inthí
	Ίνδ-ός	-ή
Irish	irlanthós	irlanthí
	Ίρλανδ-ός	-ή
Italian	italós	italítha
	Ίταλ-ός	-ίδα
Japanese	yaponézos	yaponéza
	Γιαπων-έζος	-έζα
New Zealander	neozilanthós	neozilanthí
	Νεοζηλανδ-ός	-ή
Norwegian	norvighós	norvighítha
	Νορβηγ-ός	-ίδα
Portuguese	portoghálos	portoghalítha
	Πορτογάλ-ος	-ίδα
Russian	rósos	rosítha
	Ρῶσ-ος	-ίδα
Scottish	skotsézos	skotséza
	Σκωτσέζ-ος	-α
Spanish	ispanós	ispanítha
	Ίσπαν-ός	-ίδα
Swedish	sooithós	sooithéza
	Σουηδ-ός	-έζα
Swiss	elvetós	elvetítha
	Έλβετ-ός	-ίδα
Welsh	ooalós	ooalítha
	Οὐαλλ-ός	-ίδα